THIS IS IT!

Fanfare . . . puh-*leease*! Sound the trumpets! Bang the drums! Here it is . . . the ~~~~~te guide to the most favori~~~~~~~~~~~~~~ of Nintendo®-game-~~~~~~ have all been ~~~~~~~~ most successf~~~~~~~ Nintendo games ~~~~~~~~~~~ome video screen—th~~~~~~~~IO BROS. games!

Jeff Rovin, the author of *How to Win at Nintendo Games I, II* and *III*—not to mention *How to Win at Nintendo Sports Games*—is back again with what is possibly his greatest Nintendo games book of all! While making sure that none of the mystery or enjoyment is taken away from the SUPER MARIO BROS. games, he gives you in-depth tips and analysis of each succeeding level of SUPER MARIO BROS. 1, 2, *and* 3—as well as *Super Mario Land* and the latest sensation—*Dr. Mario!*

Quite simply, this is a book no SUPER MARIO BROS. games lover worth his or her salt would want to do without. The indescribably entertaining worlds of the SUPER MARIO BROS. games will never seem quite the same!

HOW TO WIN AT SUPER MARIO BROS. GAMES

Jeff Rovin

ST. MARTIN'S PAPERBACKS

How to Win at Super Mario Bros. Games is an unofficial guide, not endorsed by Nintendo®.

Nintendo is a registered trademark of Nintendo of America Inc. Super Mario Bros., Super Mario Bros. 2, Super Mario Bros. 3, Super Mario Land, Dr. Mario and Game Boy are all trademarks of Nintendo of America, Inc.

HOW TO WIN AT SUPER MARIO BROS. GAMES

ISBN: 0-312-92656-1

Printed in the United States of America

St. Martin's Paperbacks edition/December 1990

10 9 8 7 6 5 4 3 2

CONTENTS

INTRODUCTION

Mario!

Videogame star and TV star—named, it is said, after an employee at Nintendo's U.S. headquarters—his image is on notebooks, stickers, cereal boxes, comic books—you name it.

Who'd have thought such fame awaited the feisty little carpenter when he made his videogame debut back in 1981? Then, he was the more or less anonymous nemesis of the charismatic monkey villain Donkey Kong in the Nintendo arcade (or "coin-op") game of the same name. In fact, Mario even became something of a bad guy in the arcade sequel, *Donkey Kong Jr.*, in which the player took the part of the big ape's offspring as he tried to rescue Pop from Mario's cage.

Things really began to cook for Mario when he was given his own game, *Mario Brothers*, in which he and his brother Luigi—making his videogame debut—had to clean crabs, turtles, and other vermin from a sewer system. *Mario Brothers* was popular enough to spawn a sequel, *Super Mario Brothers*, which was really a creative and commercial breakthrough: the game designers placed Mario in a fantasy land where there were opportunities to create imaginative foes, landscapes, power-ups, and a wonderfully complex quest. The game was a smash, and when Nintendo made the move into home videogames in 1985, *Super Mario Brothers* was the first cartridge produced for the new Nintendo Entertainment System.

The unassuming "Everyman" hero proved wildly popular, and sequels followed. Each of the four Mario adventures has been different, with new settings and foes—yet each game has maintained the fundamentally nonviolent charm and boundless sense of wonder that made the first Mario game so popular.

Where will it end?

It's too early to say whether Mario will join the pantheon of great media heroes like James Bond and Donald Duck, whose immortality is assured.

But he's getting there.

And speaking of *getting* somewhere—

We hope this book will help *you* get somewhere: namely, to the end of Mario's many journeys! Within these pages you'll find never-before-revealed tips and details about the games, as well as the first-ever, in-depth coverage of 1990's super-hit, *Super Mario Bros. 3.*

So—Wart are you waiting for?

Let the games begin!

SUPER MARIO LAND

Objective:

In all the world, there was no more contented realm than Sarasaland. Then, one day, a black cloud loomed overhead and the alien monster Tatanga emerged, conquering Sarasaland by hypnotizing its inhabitants. Adding insult to injury, Tatanga decided to wed Sarasaland's Princess Daisy. Enter Mario, who vows to cross the four kingdoms of Sarasaland—Birabuto (World One), Muda (Two), Easton (Three), and Chai (World Four), each of which consists of three lesser realms—to rescue Daisy before the nuptial day, defeat Tatanga, and liberate Sarasaland.

Gameplay:

Many lethal creatures work for Tatanga, and to defeat them, Mario must leap and land on top of them *or* butt them off the Blocks on which they're standing. Along the way, he obtains various power-up items. Each Heart you nab gives you an additional Mario; one hundred Coins also provides an extra Mario. (Note: most Blocks give one Coin. Some, noted below, give more—how many Coins you get from these depends entirely on *how fast you repeatedly strike the Block*). You can also get Stars, Flowers, and Super Mushrooms. Super Mushrooms increase Mario's size—that is, cause him to become "powered-up" as Super Mario—Flowers enable him to throw Super Balls at foes. (Only one Super Ball can be on the screen at a time; one Ball kills *both* parts of two-section creatures like Nokobons and Mekabons; but, sadly, some creatures, like Honen, are impervious to them.) Stars make him invincible for short periods. You'll know when your invincibility is about to run out. A theme from *Orpheus in the Underworld* plays through twice. When it ends, so does your imperviousness. Be advised, however, that you're invincible *only* when it comes to enemies: if you fall off a Ledge, you'll die. These items are all located inside ? Blocks. Blocks from which Super Mushrooms emerge when Mario is not Super Mario will give forth Flowers when he is. If you can't get these items immediately, don't panic. Unless they fall into water or off a Ledge, they remain onscreen for as long as you're in that screen. Mario also has a submarine, Marine Pop, and an airplane, Sky Pop. These are used only in Worlds 2/3 and 4/3, respectively. When you fire their guns, no more than three unexploded projectiles can appear on the screen at once.

Another power Mario possesses is manifested primarily in treasure rooms. In addition to collecting Coins, you'll be breaking Blocks in the walkways for points and power-ups; this will leave holes in the floor. (In some rooms, the Coins are already hanging over gaps in the walkway.) How, then, do you get across the gaps? Simply keep the B button pressed down. That will enable you, literally, to walk on air! This skill also works at the beginning of 2/2.

If Mario dies at any point in the game, you don't lose any of the Coins or points you've amassed, though your next Mario starts back a short distance in most cases. In a few sections of the game, he actually starts *ahead* of where he died! The No-kobon platform at the end of 2/2 is a rare example of that.) And while any foes you've killed will usually remain expired—the Honen at the start of 2/1 are an exception—the new Mario can get all the ?'s again. Likewise, any foe that may have been about to attack when you entered a Pipe, will be gone when you emerge. By the same token, before you enter any Pipe, be certain you collect any Coins or power-ups from ? Blocks to the immediate right of the Pipe. The ? will be replenished when you emerge, allowing you to "double-dip."

Finally, just in case you lose track of the time, the music will speed up when you have just 100 seconds left.

Points:

These range from 100 for each little squirt that attacks, to 5000 for the bosses of each level . . . and Tatanga. A Super (that is, "powered-up") Mario also earns 50 points for shattering Blocks; normal Mario can't shatter them. (Note: creatures that can detach body parts grant more points when killed in one piece than if each section is slain separately. Just make sure you *do* kill both parts, however, as the remaining part may regenerate what you destroyed.) Points are also awarded for each Coin collected. In every level, you're playing against time, so don't dawdle!

Strategies:

Each of Sarasaland's worlds is divided into three sections. Here's how to get through them all.

1/1: There's a Coin in the first Block, a power-up in the second, and a Coin in the third. Get on the third Pipe and press down: there's a Coin room inside. Upon emerging, collect a Coin from the Block above. (As noted above, in situations like this, if you get the Coin *before* going into the Pipe, you can hit the Block and collect again when you emerge!) Stop at the foot of the plateau ahead. There's a Chibibo on it, so stand there until the little fellow comes down, then jump on it. When you reach the first row of Blocks, either hurry to the right before the two Chibibos drop from the Ledge, or stay to the left until they emerge from under the row. If *you're* underneath, the Blocks will prevent you from jumping and stomping the creatures, and you'll perish. (Unless, of course, you've shattered the Blocks and can jump up in the narrow channel. However, it's a tricky move and not worth the risk.)

After dispensing with the twerps, get the Coin in the ? above. Beyond the next Pipe is a row of six Blocks. Hop on them, go to the right, then jump down and get the Coins as you fall. If you miss them, get on the ?, smash all the Blocks on the upper left, leap back onto the Pipe—assuming you haven't scrolled it too far left—and try again. (If you fail at this, wait till you get Super Ball power across the Pit and shoot left to nail the Coins.) When you're underneath the row, collect the Coin from the lonely ?, then jump onto that Block and hit the row above: the second Block from right contains a 1-Up. Jump onto the row of three Blocks to the right, hop up and hit the ? on top, then leap onto it and get the power-up. (If you're Super Mario, make sure that you don't inadvertently smash the Blocks below the ? before you use them as stepping-stones! Otherwise, you won't be able to get the power-up.)

A Nokobon comes next; jump on it then get away *fast*, or its Bomb will explode. Obtain a Coin from the ? after the Pipe, at which point you'll arrive at three rows of Blocks. None on bottom can be broken, so don't bother trying. Just hop onto the second row, collect Coins from all the top Blocks, drop back down to the bottom row, then butt all the Blocks in the second row for Coins. Leap the Pit:

the Pipe there takes you to a Coin room. (Remember: first get the Coin in the ? to the right.) If you're a non–Super Mario, bounce off the ceiling as you go along the bottom tier—that is, press the controller right and keep jabbing the A button repeatedly—this will save a lot of time. When you leave the room, there are Coins in the next two ? Blocks. As soon as the second ? appears, a Fly will come after you. Flies hop, then rest for several seconds; jump on top of them immediately after they hop. Next up is a Pipe to the left of a stack of Blocks. Jump onto the Pipe, using a Super Ball on the Chibibo down there—or jump down on it if you don't have Super Ball power—then hop onto the stack. Wait there, and shoot the Chibibo when it approaches. Now jump, hit the ?, and grab Star when it floats down. (If you'd hit the ? *before* blasting the second Chibibo, the Star would have drifted down right on top of it. Where would you be then?) Invincible, you can race ahead.

The next row of Blocks is all Coins. If you missed catching the Star, watch out, again, that you don't get trapped underneath as a Chibibo enters from the right. The next two ?'s have Coins. Your invincibility should carry you through the first Fly that attacks . . . and, if you hurry, the second as well. If not, kill them as before. (Regarding the first Fly: if you've run out of invincibility, you can stand atop the Pipe. When the Fly jumps up at you, it will *usually* self-destruct.) Get the ? (a Coin).

The Sphinx on the other side of the Pit can't hurt you, so just hop over. Above it you'll find a row in which the last (unmarked) Block contains many Coins; you can get up to 15 if you strike *fast*. Just keep butting the Block until it's empty. At the pyramid-like structure made of Blocks, get the lower row of Coins first. (If you get the upper row first, the screen will scroll to the left so far that you may not be able to get back down to them.) If you're Super Mario and thus oversized, simply stand on the first Block on the left of the lowest Coin row—*not* the Block jutting to the left, below it—squat, and fire a Super Ball at the Coins. The Ball will collect them for you! Go up to the second row and squat *squarely* on the Block at the beginning of the second tier of Coins. Fire a Super Ball to collect the Coins. If you have trouble with that, you can always try for the second row by getting behind the Pyramid, leaping down—which you'll do to collect the string of Coins floating there—and shooting to the left at the Coins.

Upon reaching the Tower at the end of the level, use the Elevators to get into the door at top. (Note: you can stand directly underneath the Elevators at the end of many levels and jump *up* onto them, instead of leaping from the sides. The advantage to this is that you can position yourself so that you'll be at the very edge of the Elevator when you leap on, already facing toward the right. If you have to waste time positioning yourself *after* you're on the Elevator, your fine-tuning may cause you to miss your ideal jump-off time.) Entering the Tower on top, you'll access a bonus stage: there, you must press the A button as if the controller were a slot machine. If your timing is right, you'll win a good many extra lives! If you enter the Tower's bottom door, you get diddly! Because of that fact, if time threatens to run out when you're near the very end of a level, it's better to *let* it do so than to compromise and go in the bottom. At worst, you'll gain back the life you lost by going in the top door. At best, you'll add two lives to your storehouse of Marios—three, minus the one you sacrificed.

1/2: When you come to the first three Blocks, get the ? last if you're not Super Mario; inside is a power-up which you'll have to chase as it falls to the level below. While you're on the next platform, be aware that the Chibibo isn't bound to its platform to the right; it can come down and get you. Your next foes will be a pair of Bunbuns: Spear-dropping Flies. You can leap on top of these to kill them, or you can simply wait until each drops a Spear and then dash under it. There's plenty of time to do so. The next ? is a Coin, after which you'll cross five platforms. (Watch it—there's a pair of Nokobons here, so hit them with Super Balls or pound on them and scurry before their Bombs go off.)

After dispatching a Chibibo, you'll reach a row of Blocks with a Coin in the center—and a Nokobon on top; butt the Block and it'll fall off. Look down, to the right, and you'll see a ?. Jump down . . . but shift Mario so that he lands to the *left* of this. Then, carefully, move to the far left of the platform—don't move *too* far left, though, or you'll drop off the side—and leap up. There's an Invisible Block here. Hit it and you'll release a 1-Up. Catch it, get the Coin from the ?, then jump up on the ? Block to get to the platform to the right. There are a pair of Elevators: when you leap from the Elevator on the right, do so when it's quite high; that way, you can gather the loose change hanging in the air on your way down.

More Bunbuns attack moments later: two in the air, a third high in the air, a fourth flying very low. You can jump on the first, second, and fourth; to kill the third, rebound a Super Ball off the ground. At the Pyramid, watch for the two Chibibos coming down, then climb to the top and get the ?, a power-up. (You'll have to scoot to the right, to the lowest Ledge on that side, to catch it. Just make sure you don't scoot *off* the edge of the Pyramid!) There's a trio of Elevators to the right: take them fast and you'll be in good position to get the Coins to the right; that is, a rapid crossing will place you on the third Elevator while it's high. Immediately go to the far right of the Ledge you're on, so that you're standing just under the Ledge with the Nokobon (don't worry: the Bomb-toting Turtle won't come down at you). Another Bunbun will attack, but you'll be safe from its Spears here. When the flying fiend leaves, jump up, either killing or avoiding the Nokobon. The next row of Blocks contains a Coin, a 1-Up, and a Coin, in that order. There's a Coin in the ? below, but no Invisible Block this time.

At the next Elevator—there's just one this time—jump to the right in such a way that you can gather the three horizontal Coins on your way to Ledge.

Two Bunbuns attack in tandem; stand as if the last tree on the right were passing through you, and their shafts won't touch you. Fire to the *right* as each one is leaving: your projectile will ricochet to the left and kill them. When you reach the final Elevator, just before the Tower, once again go for the top door and the bonus stage. There are two Blocks hanging in the air to the right of the Elevator, and you must use these as stepping-stones to get into the Tower. Thing is, you've got to get on and off them super fast: they fall apart in less than a second. You won't die if you drop, but you won't be able to get into the top door. Don't lose heart it one of the fragile Blocks falls: you can still get in with just a single Block. The trick is to stand on the very edge of the Elevator and jump as soon as it's lined up with the word "Battery" on the left side of the Game Boy.

1/3: Whatever you do on this level, don't lose your power-up ability. Much of the treasure here requires Block-bashing ability. To begin with, go *left*, so that you're standing just to the right of the wall there! Jump up, and you'll uncover a secret Elevator above your head! When you do so, clear out the Coins from the ?'s on the right—taking care not to scroll the Elevator off the left side—then go back to the Block on the left side of the row, get on top of it, jump left to the Elevator, and ride it to a secret cache of Coins—28 beauties in all! You'll miss out on the wonderful things below, like Falling Rocks and Pakkun Flowers, but try not to be disappointed!

When you reach the edge of the upper Ledge, look down. Wait until the Pakkun Flower retreats into the Pipe below you, then jump in. (This Pakkun stays down for a long time, so there's no need to hurry.) Once inside, go to the middle level, smash the Blocks above, go down, break the Blocks below that, then drop to the floor and bust up the Blocks there. You'll get the points *and* be able to cross the gaps and collect the Coins by pressing down the B button. Note: the second breakable Block from the right, on the bottom, contains many Coins. Just keep hitting it!

Leap the Pit when you emerge, and you'll come to four Pipes. The first two don't contain Pakkuns, but the second two do. Get on the second Pipe, wait until the Pakkun Flower goes down on the third, leap onto it, then vault over the fourth Pipe entirely. There are Coins in the row of ? Blocks you'll encounter overhead, but watch out: stop under the first ? on the left and then *immediately* back away to the left. Falling Rocks will drop just beyond that. Stand still till they stop, then get the Coins. There are more Coins in the next row of Blocks overhead, but they won't be as easy to get since a Gao is guarding them. If you have Super Balls, run ahead, stand beneath the left torch, just to the right of it; fire, run back to the left. The Ball will ricochet and eventually hit the Gao. If you *don't* have Super Balls, wait until the monster fires, then hurry onto the row of Blocks and jump down on the creature.

Watch out, though: Gao can shoot up as well as down, so don't think you're immune just because you're above the creature! In either case, crack the Blocks and bop the ?'s when the menace is ended. When you're finished, go *back* to the empty space where you destroyed the Block on the right—the space to the left of the ? on the far right. Hit up again, at the empty space. Another secret Elevator will appear! Hop on, and it will lift you to a Pipe the top of which has a very well-stocked Coin room! After collecting the Coins on the bottom, break the Blocks immediately overhead and gather 24 Coins in there. To reach the ones on top, you'll need to fire a Super Ball. Climb on the exit Pipe to get the foursome above it, then leave.

There's nothing in the small Pyramid that follows. When you get over it, hop onto the lowest tier, which contains Coins. If you're Super Mario, jump up, shattering the Blocks ahead, and get the Coins from the ?'s. (Don't worry: the Nokobon can't leave its Ledge.) When that's done, hop up and use a Super Ball against the Turtle, then get the Coins on that tier. If you have the time, press down on the controller so that Mario is squatting, then press A repeatedly so he can shimmy down the tunnel, collecting Coins. If you are running out of time, just stay on the Ledge where you killed the Nokobon, go right, leap over the wall, turn, squat and fire a Super Ball left down the middle walkway to collect the Coins. Stand. Jump into the right angle formed by the Blocks above you—the vertex is in the upper-left corner—and an Invisible Block will appear. Hit it repeatedly for Coins. Head right, over the Pyramid, after pausing to make sure the Falling Blocks there have already fallen!

Now, then—remember, above, where we said, "If you're Super Mario . . ."? If you're *not*, all is not lost! Instead of busting the wall, fighting the Nokobon, and so forth, just squat and go right along the lowest passageway. This gives you access to the Pyramid laden with Coins. Just don't go rushing in, though: those Falling Rocks mentioned in the last paragraph will welcome you as you enter the treasure chamber! There's also a power-up in here. When you reach the other side of the Pyramid, shatter the Blocks to get out. You'll come to a pair of Sphinxes beneath a double row of Blocks: smash them all and acquire a power-up. Leap the Bridge that lies just beyond it, or you'll plunge to oblivion.

As soon as you get to the other side, stop: a Gao is lurking on the far right, spitting fireballs, though they can't get you if you stand where you are. Just wait until it's fired one, then charge! You'll be able to pounce on it before it gets off another shot. Immediately after fighting one more Gao, you'll face King Totomesu, the boss of the level. It'll take five Super Balls to kill him; straddle the fourth and fifth Blocks from the left, leap his first fireball, and shoot on the way down. If you have no Super Balls, you must leap over the creature; as soon as the music changes, run to the right as fast as you can. Jump its first fireball, then run under its second. There's a brief interval before the next two-fireball sequence: run *right up to its nose* and jump over the

boss . . . making sure, when you do, that you clear
the creature's tail. You're trying to land in the
small space behind it, not on the monster itself.
(And don't try to kill the beast by landing on its
head, as you can do with lesser Gaos—you'll die.)
Once you leap the monster, it'll explode. (Another
option: if you're Super Mario but have no Super
Balls, you can run right *through* the monster. You'll
lose your power-up, but if time is running out, it *is*
a viable choice!) Step up to the stone barrier behind
the creature, and the wall will come down. You'll
enter a chamber where Daisy will appear . . . but
only to tantalize you! She'll turn into a Fly and
vanish after a moment, and you'll have to proceed
to—

2/1: There are Coins in the ?'s in the first row of
Blocks. After that, jump down along the right wall
of the plateau on which you're standing. Notice
where the Honen is leaping from the water, then
stand on top of that spot. It will perish when it hits
the bottom of your feet. Hop up two plateaus and
dispatch the next Honen in this fashion, collect the
Coins above, then hop back to the left, down two
plateaus. Now jump onto the bottom plateau to the
right and stand on the left side. Jump up and you'll
uncover an Invisible Block with a power-up. Leap
onto the Block and pluck the Flower. If it's a Super
Mushroom, you can't catch it while standing anywhere on that Ledge; you're going to have to nab it
while leaping to the Ledge to the right. Otherwise,
it'll fall in the water.

Continue to the right. After crossing the two Elevators, get the power-up from the ? to the right of the Pipe, shoot Super Balls to get the Coins to the right, then drop down the Pipe. Once inside, step onto the platform on the floor, just to your right. Hit the uppermost block, which is *attached to the wall to your immediate right*. You'll get a power-up. Don't pluck it . . . yet. Go to the left of the platform, hop onto the row of two Blocks and, from there, jump up onto the single Block above. Leap up and smash the Block that leads into the upper cache. (Note: if you accidentally break one of the stepping-stones while leaping up, that's not good . . . but it isn't necessarily disastrous if you have Super Ball power. Crack the Block that leads to the upstairs section anyway, go to the bottom section, and we'll tell you what to do in a moment.) Jump up and collect all but the rightmost row of Coins up here. Go to the wall on the right, carefully snatching or Super Balling the top two Coins— leaving the two below it untouched—then leave this area. Obliterate all the breakable Blocks on the left side, then go to the bottom section and gather the Coins there. When you're finished, get on top of the exit Pipe, leap up to obtain the two remaining Coins, and leave. If you were unable to get into the Coin room above, *don't* leave until you've turned left on top of the exit Pipe, squatted, and fired a Super Ball. It will ricochet into the room and clean out all but one or two of the Coins.

Outside, you'll collect Coins on several plateaus, then come to a series of Bridges with Coins along

the top. You can avoid the Honen using a stop-and-
go technique, or you can watch where they emerge
and stand on top of them as before, killing them
when they pop up. At the end of the first Bridge,
wait until the Nokobon comes along on the second.
Jump up and Super Ball it. If you don't have Super
Ball power, wait until it turns and is headed right
before proceeding. If you leap on it and kill it right
away, you may run into a Honen leaping right beside it while fleeing the Turtle's Bomb.

As you continue ahead, deal with the Honen as
described above. Keep an eye out for the pair of
Chibibos that arrive in tandem. If you jump on the
first, be sure you jump again *immediately* on the
second, or it'll run into you and kill you. Don't simply leap ahead to avoid them. Even though they'll
wander to the left and drop off the Ledge like little
lemmings, you may jump right into the Honen rising and falling on the right! In the row of Blocks to
the right, you'll find a Coin in the left and a Star
in the right. You'll have to leap to the right to catch
the latter as it emerges. Be careful: a Chibibo has
wandered onto the plateau below, so make sure you
land on its head as you fall.

Run quickly while you're invincible, and you'll
be able to get past the fire-breathing Yurarin: it'll
attack right after the fourth plateau beyond the
floating Coins. This creature turns to fire at you
once you pass, so don't pause to take a breath just
because you got around it! (Whether you caught the
Star or not, it's a good idea to make the Pipe your
goal; as soon as you've made it by the Yurarin, take

a big leap over the Pipe and press yourself against the Pipe's right side. The Yurarin's fireball won't get you there.)

The next Pipe is another Coin room. Before entering, go to the ? on the top right: multiple Coins can be found here. When you do enter the Pipe, you might be inclined to panic: after clearing the Coins off the floor, you'll notice that there doesn't seem to be any way out! Fear not. Go to the bottom right corner and jump up. This will reveal an Invisible Block which will enable you to leap up to the Coins *and* get out. Use the B button technique described earlier to cross the gaps in the walkways. However, on the lower walkway, stop before you reach the last gap or you *will* fall through it. You won't perish, but you'll waste time getting back up there. Note that you can smash the Blocks directly below the Pipe exit above.

Upon emerging, again use repeated hits to get the Coins from the ? Block above, gather the floating Coins to the right, and pluck a Coin and power-up from the left and right, respectively, of the row of Blocks above. Immediately after this row, you'll face a Yurarin. Jump its fireballs and position yourself on the Bridge so that the killer will come up under your feet and die. If you don't, you've got a problem: a second Yurarin pops up to the right, and if the other one is still on your left, you'll be caught in a dangerous crossfire. If this happens, leap their fireballs while edging to the right. (Do this even if you've killed the first Yurarin ... though facing one is obviously a whole lot easier!)

Wait until it's fired, then run to the right and jump
over it, onto the Ledge to the left of the Elevator.
If you time your jump right, you'll have the unpar-
alleled satisfaction of actually grazing the Yurarin's head on your way over, killing it . . . a neat
bonus.) Once the Yurarin is off the screen, it'll no
longer fire at you. Get on the Elevator, stand on
the left side, and as the Elevator is rising, bust the
Block and the ? Block above: in it is a 1-Up. You'll
have to break them both *and* jump to the Coin
Ledge on the right before the Elevator descends:
the 1-Up falls onto the Ledge and keeps rolling; if
you don't get to the Ledge immediately, the 1-Up
will fall away. Get the 1-Up and Coins both, then
leap onto the top of the wall to the right and take
a hefty jump onto the Elevator. (Note: if you're not
Super Mario, you can't get the 1-Up because you
can't break the Block underneath it. Sorry.) Make
a quick leap onto the platform by the Tower door
and enter on top.

2/2: Your first foe here is a Mekabon, which de-
taches its Head and sends it soaring down at you.
Luckily, it isn't a homing head. As soon as you start
the round, rush right, get on the Ledge, and jump
on the Head before it comes off. If you fail at this,
you can attack the Head and body separately or
simply stay out the Head's way. When it reattaches
itself to the body, leap up and come down on top of
it. So long Mekabon. Use the B button to run across
the string of Blocks and gaps to the right. There's
a power-up in the first Block; it'll drift to the right,

and you'll have to jump to catch it. Make sure that when you do, you land on top of the wall *or* on the Chibibo waiting for you. You'll find a Coin in the second ?. Before you can crawl down the Pipe, it will be necessary to kill the Nokobon on top. Jump onto the Block to the left of the Pipe, and either fire at or hop on the Turtle to kill it. If you did the latter, quickly leap back to the Block on the left or onto either side of the platform on which the Pipe is resting, to avoid the Bomb. When it detonates, get on the Pipe, hop up to grab the Coins above, then drop down.

In the Pipe, the uppermost Block on the wall immediately to your right contains multiple Coins. As you did in the 2/1 treasure room of this design, take care not to shatter any Blocks. Follow the same procedure here as you did there. Leaving the Pipe, get the Coin in the ? to the left (again), then collect the Coins above and head right. There's a Coin in the next two ?'s, and then a pair of Elevators; climb onto the ? you last hit to board the horizontal transports. However, be alert: when you leap off the second (last) Elevator, jump high so you can sweep up the vertical line of Coins to the right. As you fall, shift to the left so you land on the Pipe and not on the Nokobon to its right. If you land on the creature, get onto the Pipe *fast* or you'll blow up!

If you're not Super Mario and you don't want to face the robot to the right, just hop to the stone Ledge on the right, then step off to the left; an invisible walkway extends slightly over the water. Proceed on the lower level. Harvest all the Coins

here, facing only minimal opposition from a trio of
Chibibos. Deal with these by staying to the left side
of any tunnel in which they appear, just to the left
of the column: that's the only area where there's
room enough for you to jump. Wait for them to return to the left before making a leap onto their nog-
gins. (Note: if you choose to go across the top, stand
on the Ledge to the upper right of the Pipe, wait
until the Mekabon's head reattaches, then leap up
and attack it. Up here, you won't get nearly as
many Coins, but you *will* find a Star in the last
Block on the right of the first overhead row. Cross
on top, kill the Mekabon below you at the other
end, then jump down and get the Star.) Your relatively safe passage ends when you come to a Nokobon waiting for you on the other side. Wait until
it starts walking right before you jump over. A Chibibo will attack; leap on it, then kill the Nokobon
and dodge the fireballs of one of your old friends, a
Yurarin, who's rising and falling on the right. Using the Blocks on the ground to shield you from the
flame-spitter, leap when the monster goes down,
timing the jump to hit its head when he rises: otherwise, you'll have it breathing flame at your back
while you deal with the Mekabon that arrives on
the right.

After crowning the robot—head and body both,
remember, or it'll regenerate—you'll come to a pair
of Elevators, the first one moving vertically, the
second horizontally. When you reach the row of
Blocks with a single Block above it, hit them all for
Coins. Mind you, the Nokobon and Yurarin to the

right may have something to say about that: so, when you leave the Elevator, jump onto the Ledge as the Nokobon is walking to the right. Walk with it. When it turns left, you turn left as well: when you clear the leftmost ?, jump up, land on the Turtle, then run to the right under the row of ?'s to avoid the blast. Clear out the ?'s, then, between fireballs from the Yurarin, climb up and get the Coin from the ? on top. Jump down onto the big Block to the right—the fireballs can't touch you here—then time your jump to kill the Yurarin as you leap to the Block on the right. If you fail at this, hurry and get behind the Block to the right of the Pipe, where you'll be safe. Kill the Chibibo below you, get the Coin from the ?, then wait until the Pakkun Flower in the Pipe to the right sinks away. When it does, hop on, get the Coins above, and slide into the Pipe. Clean the Coins from the bottom, then stand just to the left of the leftmost Block of the second row. Jump up to uncover the Invisible Block here, and ascend. Make sure you don't leave before butting the left Block under the exit Pipe: there are multiple Coins here.

Exit, get the Coin in the ? to the left, grab the Coins above, and hop on the Blocks to go right. Hit the ? for a Coin, then climb onto that Block and try and hop to the Elevator which shifts from side to side. (Miracles happen!) This leads to the top door. More than likely, you'll have to take the Block staircase. Be *real* quick about it: each Block collapses the instant you step on it! There is no bonus stage at the end of this round.

2/3: This level is all water and it scrolls *by itself*—you just go along with the flow. Stay mostly toward the left of the screen, darting ahead to sweep up the Coins, then getting back. If you're Super Mario, look for existing gaps in walls; that's less you'll have to shoot in order to fit through. Blast Yurarins the *instant* they appear: their fireballs are deadly, even underwater. Torion will not only come at you from the right, they'll turn if you haven't shot them and come at you again from the left (though only once). Don't shoot or touch the Gunions: they won't bother you if you don't bother them. Touch them, and you die; hit them with projectiles, and they split in two and attack. Also, if you get to the left of a Block and you get scrolled into the left side of the screen, you'll perish.

Pay attention to your surroundings, there are items to collect: a power-up in the first collection of Blocks on top, and, perhaps most importantly, a Star in the second set of Blocks on the bottom. Just make sure you're quick once you uncover it. Being so close to the bottom of the water, the Star is swallowed up quickly by the sands. When you obtain invincibility, hurry to the far right, shooting ahead. (Remember: you're impervious as long as the song runs!) When the last bars of music sound, return to the left. Upon reaching the first Column which has a narrow channel in the bottom, blast the lower four Blocks to get a power-up. You can really rack up the Coins when you come to the region where they spell MARIO—just sweep up and down on the left; no enemy will bother you here. And blast just below the midsection of the Column ahead for a Heart. (If you want a big advantage here, do something to kill yourself after you get the 1-Up. You'll come back to life *before* the MARIO Coin section, and will be able to add as many lives as you want to your collection!) Watch for the last (fourth) Column in this series of Columns: the top section contains a power-up. Note: on this level, if you're Mario and you run up against a wall of Blocks, you need only clear out one tier to get through. Super Mario requires two. That *can* be a handicap if you're busy fending off fish. Note: any projectiles fired by creatures, such as Yurarin, do *not* disintegrate when the monster dies. Keep an eye on these while you're battling the source! These can be especially dangerous while you're passing through channels in the Blocks: if they enter the other side while you're inside, you're cooked!

You'll be battling Tamao and Dragonzamasu at the end of this realm. Tamao is a blob that cannot be destroyed. Thus, all you can do is avoid it. While so doing, you must also fire at its boss, behind it. Dragonzamasu spits fireballs that have to be dodged while you shoot at the creature. It takes 20 hits to destroy Dragonzamasu ... though, fortunately, it isn't necessary to slay it. When Dragonzamasu rises, get behind the Block in front of it—you can use this Block for protection from the boss's fire when he's down; it can't hit you here, though Tamao can. Shoot the three Blocks of the bottom row to the right. Dart into the narrow tunnel you've created. When Dragonzamasu rises again, slide to the left and rise slightly, knock out the three Blocks on the row above it, and pilot your ship on into the opening to win the round

3/1: When the Batadon arrives—which it does, instantly—shift to the left. It will fly in that direction, at which point you must run to the right, jump on the Pipe, get the Coin, and leap over the Pit . . . all before the Batadon flies right. There's a Nokobon at the second Pipe, but that won't present a prob lem. There are two rows of Blocks, and a power-up in the rightmost Block on the top. Get it, then leap quickly across the Bridge that follows, since it will collapse beneath you. Land on the Nokobon on the other side, then watch out when leaping onto the Pipe to get the Coin in the Block on the right: a Cannon that fires Gira is in the next Pipe to the right. You can step on the projectile to stop it . . . but, frankly, it's less risky to avoid it altogether. Just time your progress so that you can get on top of the Cannon Pipe when the Cannon is submerged. (Note: you can stand on a Pipe when the Cannon comes up, and rise on top of it. You can also stand to one side or the other on the Pipe and not be hurt when a Gira is launched. What you *can't* do is try to get up while the Cannon is firing!) Slip down the Pipe, getting the Coins by leaping over the Spikes *carefully*.

When you emerge, get to the ? on the top right: there are multiple Coins in here. Unfortunately, a Batadon guards it. When the creature is to the right—and this strategy goes for all the Batadons you'll face on this level—leap onto the Z-shaped Ledge to the left, above you. (You can't hide under that Ledge: it'll get you there, even though it looks as though the creature can't fit!) Step on the Batadon's head when it comes after you. (Note: if the Batadon kills you, take heart in the fact that it won't be there when you go to your next Mario.) You can get up to 17 Coins from the Block above! You'll have to kill the Nokobon to the Ledge on the right in order to get to the Elevators. Upon reaching them, note that the middle one is extremely narrow, so don't jump with your usual abandon. You'll find a Pakkun Flower in the next Pipe, and a Nokobon on the Column to its right. This is tricky: if you don't have Super Balls, you must to hop from the Elevator onto the Turtle, then *immediately* jump onto the Column to its right *or* back to the Pipe—if the Pakkun is submerged—to avoid the explosion. In either case, leap onto the Turtle *only* when it's on the left side of the Column, or you'll perish. Use Super Balls, if you have them, to reap the Coins floating between the Columns as you jump overhead.

After the Columns, you'll find a Pakkun Flower in the first Pipe and a Cannon in the second. Hop over the first, wait until the Cannon goes down, then jump onto the Cannon Pipe and continue on your way, making sure you collect the Coins from the Blocks overhead. Be prepared to face your first Tokotoko; the wonderfully animated stone head runs at you, rattling its fist. You can stop it by jumping onto its Head or simply leaping it and letting it run past. A second Tokotoko will drop down at you from the Ledge to the left of the vertical Column of floating Coins. As soon as it does so, another Batadon will attack. Bop the Tokotoko before the winged creature arrives, then deal with it as you did the first one you faced—the landscape is virtually identical. Collect the Column of Coins, then climb the Blocks to the right, drop down, and jump up to get a Coin from the ?. You'll be standing on another Z-shaped Ledge. Climb down to the Ledge on the right, jump up, and you'll uncover an Invisible Block with a Heart. You'll have to leap the Pit to the right to catch it ... and, when you do, it's important that you drop down through the gap to the Ledge below as *fast as possible*, since a very dogged Batadon will show up within moments. Go back to the Z-shaped Ledge and kill it as you did before. (Here's an alternate plan you can try: before hitting the Invisible Block, step onto the Ledge to the right of the Z-shaped Ledge and go to the right edge. That'll bring on the Batadon. Carefully walk back to the left and *step* up onto the Z-shaped Ledge. Don't jump back up onto that Ledge, or you'll bump into the Invisible Block and uncover the Heart; with the Batadon there, you'll never be able to get it. Kill the Batadon as before, and then uncover the Heart.)

Upon the creature's demise, climb to the right, stomp the Nokobon, collect the floating Coins in the vertical Column, then jump down onto the vertically shifting Elevator. Transfer to the horizontal one, mindful of the fact that there's a Cannon in the Pipe beyond, and one in the Pipe beyond that . . . so you'll have two of them firing at you while you're still on the Elevator! Leap onto the Giras as they pass, to destroy them, or simply hop over them, then jump on the first Pipe when the Cannon goes down. Hit the Block above for a power-up, then leap onto the second Pipe when the Cannon's down, and *be on your toes*! Jump off and *rush* ahead to the Ledge beyond, the one on which the Pipe is sitting—it's a row of Blocks comprised of ?'s. A trio of Tokotokos comes rushing along, only *these* Heads turn once they reach the left side of the screen and attack again! If you're on the left side of the Ledge, you can jump down and bop them. If you're *really* good, you can actually graze the Heads of at least two of the Tokotokos as you leap onto the Ledge, killing them. Once the running Heads are defeated, leap immediately onto the Coin Ledge to the left, so that you can be above the Batadon when it arrives. You'll be able to leap down on it, then go under the Pipe Ledge, bash the ?'s, and collect the Coins. Take care not to get hit by the Cannon in the *next* Pipe, and also keep an eye out for the two Batadons and more Tokotokos which attack.

Surviving these, you face an even tougher challenge: Ganchan riding. The Ganchan are boulders that come rolling at you from the right. They'll kill you if you let them . . . but they're also your ticket over the Spike fields that follow. (Note: the instructions refer to the Spikes as "Needles." Sorry, but somebody needs glasses! Those deadly shafts are fat

and tapered; something must have gotten lost in
the translation from Japanese.) Go to the edge of
the Block wall where the Spike fields begin. Stand
facing right, with Mario's foot *over* the edge of the
wall, on thin air. When the rock comes along, it
will go under your foot, pick you up, and carry you
through the air. As soon as you reach a wall of
Blocks, however, make sure you get off or you'll
perish. (If you fall on Spikes as Super Mario, hop
off quickly and you'll survive.) Position yourself on
that wall as you did on the previous one, with a
foot over the side, and hitch a ride on the next Ganchan. Repeat until you come to a Ledge shaped like
an inverted L in the air. Get on the left (lower) side
of the Ledge, and wait until the Ganchan has come
down. If you stand on the right side, this rock won't
give you a lift—it'll kill you! As soon as the boulder
has rolled down at the Ledge, leap to the right, *on
top* of the object. Ride it to the wall and get off before it sinks down into a Pit. Leap the Spikes to the
fat, horizontal Ledge laden with Coins. When
you've cleared these away, leap onto one of the
Ganchan which will materialize on the upper right.
Ride it to the Elevator, and hop from this into the
top of the Tower. If you missed that Coin Ledge,
don't worry, you can proceed along the bottom. Just
hop from the small outcrops, over the Spikes, to the
Tower at the end. These leaps are relatively easy
to make, provided you start *at once*. Those Ganchans that materialize at the right begin bouncing
in your direction. Nor do they disappear. They'll
keep rolling left and right where you have to jump,

making your passage difficult, to say the least!
However: let *one* appear. Allow it to roll after you
until you reach the Tower. Then: hop on top of it,
ride it to the Elevator, and leap up into the bonus
room.

3/2: In the early going, the most dangerous foe
you'll face are the Suu: spiders that resemble the
Stalactites in which they hide, making them tough
to spot while you're looking out for other foes! Still,
they're easy enough to avoid if spotted: if you inch
forward, you'll trigger the arachnid's descent. All
you need do, then, is quickly back up a bit, wait
until the Suu goes up again—as Hemingway said,
"The Suu Always Rises"—then rush ahead.
   The first Suu falls after the third Pipe. (There's
nothing in these Pipes, so don't bother checking.)
After you pass it, you'll face a Nokobon. Bop it and
clear the ?'s overhead: all contain Coins. There's
another Suu and Nokobon ahead—easily dealt
with—followed by a Pipe with a pair of Suus beyond
it. "Trigger" the Suu on the left by getting onto the
Pipe and dropping down to its right—but not *so* far
right that you're under the Suu! When the spider
on the left has started up, run ahead; you'll clear
the second Suu before it drops. (If you want to
kill them, wait until they're down and then jump on
their backs.) There's a Pakkun Flower in the next
Pipe: when the plant retreats, get on the Pipe and
stand there until the Suu beyond it has come down.
Leap onto the Block in the Waterfall, and from
there onto the Coin Ledge. Sweep up the money

and stop on the right side of the Ledge: a different
kind of spider, a Kumo, makes its debut here, hopping along like the Flies of 1/1. As soon as it's below the Ledge, fall onto its back, killing the
creature.

Hop onto the Column to the right to trigger the
Suu, then proceed to the next Coin Ledge ...
watching out for the Suu overhead. Get below the
Ledge and hit the last Block on the right for a
power-up. Continuing to the right, you'll find a Coin
in the Block overhead. Cross the Waterfall by hopping the Blocks, then *quickly* dispose of the Nokobon on the Ledge. A Kumo will arrive almost at
once, and if you have to deal with it and the Nokobon, you'll have your hands (and feet) full. This
Kumo will attack you on the Ledge where you're
standing, so be ready to leap up and land on top of
it. When you've killed the beasts and cleared away
the Coins, get beneath the Ledge. Break the Blocks
as you did back in 1/3 to reveal a hidden Elevator.
Ride it to the top and jump *left*—using the A button;
don't try walking on air with the B button or you'll
fall. Enter the Pipe and collect the 100 Coins
therein. There's also a power-up in the ?, which you
may need to break Blocks in this treasure room.
when you leave the Pipe, gather the Coins to the
left, then drop off the Ledge.

When you continue to the right, it'll be necessary
to leap onto a thin Column. If that weren't difficult
enough, you have to get off it *immediately*: a Sta-
lactite will fall, killing you if you linger more than
a moment. (When you jump onto the Column, make

sure that the Nokobon on the Ledge beyond is
headed to the right. Otherwise, you'll hop onto the
Column and then to the Ledge, where you'll land
on the Bomb-bearing sucker!) After killing the Nokobon, you'll have to get past a pair of Suu. Wait
until the first one comes down, then leap on its
back. You can't wait until it rises and then jump:
the arc of your leap will carry you right into the
creature's furry legs. Run over the second Suu as
well, kill the Nokobon on the Ledge, wait there for
the Kumo to arrive, jump on it, then leap to the
right, clear the Coins from the Ledge, cross the Waterfall, and get the power-up from the single overhead Block ... watching out for the Gira being
launched by the Cannon in the Pipe to the right.
Hop the Cannon—or get on top of it and then leap
to the other side—and hug the right side of the Pipe:
there's a Suu overhead, waiting to drop. When it
retreats, clear the Coins from the Blocks overhead.

After crossing the Waterfall, you'll encounter a
Kumo on the first Ledge. Be on your guard so you
land on it! (Incidentally, you'll find with this and
most previous Kumos that if you position yourself
beneath the 10's numeral of your Coin counter,
you'll be in an ideal position to jump onto the creature.) Cross the other Ledges (no problem!) and
you'll find yourself at a Spike Pit—keep an eye out
for a Block with multiple Coins here. Ride the Ganchan across ... only on this level, you have to leap
onto the boulder to get aboard. To time your leap
right, wait until the rock has hit the Spikes and
has just begun its ascent toward the left before

jumping. Get off, leap onto the next Ganchan to cross another Spike Pit, then watch out: there's a world of trouble awaiting you on the other side. You'll face a Cannon in the next Pipe, a Kumo on the other side, and a Suu above. But all is not as bleak as it seems: when you leave the rock, hug the left side of the Pipe. Get on top of the Cannon—that will trigger the Suu—leap the ugly arachnid when it descends (and when the Kumo is on the right), then crush the Kumo when you come down. A snap! If you opt to go down that Pipe, you'll find a multiple Coin Block near the center of the treasure room. Also: if you don't want to go Spike hopping, you can access the lower row of Coins by getting at them from below. Even if you're not Super Mario, you can hit these Blocks and get the bottom row of Coins. Ride the Elevators to the right—taking care not to die when bopping the Nokobon on the Ledge between them, *and* making sure you jump from the left Elevator when it's low or you'll expire when you hit the Stalactites above—and you'll come to those same fragile Blocks you've had to deal with at the end of the last few levels . . . except that if you fail to cross *these*, you won't just lose out on the top room of a Tower. You'll perish! The trick here is *not* to step on each one. There are two Blocks, then a solid Ledge, then another two Blocks. Leap on the second one from the left, quickly hop to the solid Ledge, then jump *not* onto the next Block but onto the one beyond it. Leap off at once. If any of the Blocks after this one collapse before you can get off them, you'll land on solid ground below, which leads directly to the Tower. You won't get to the top room . . . but you won't perish, either!

3/3: After you pass a Pipe and two Columns, you're going to face five tricky Elevators: the first, third, and fifth slide from side to side; the second and fourth shift diagonally to the upper right and left, respectively. To cross: when you reach the first Column, do *not* jump at once onto the first Elevator. Wait until it comes back a second time. In quick succession, go from it to the second to the third, then stop. Wait until the fourth comes near, then go to it and then onto the last one rapidly. When you hop from the last one, watch out: a Ganchan comes rolling along. Jump over it. Collect the Coins from atop the Pipe, cross a Column, and get onto the Elevator. Do *not* jump onto the Column to the right. Rather, ride the Elevator up and jump quickly onto and off the collapsible Blocks and over to the Pipe. Just make sure you time your move so that you land on the Pipe when the Pakkun Flower is down. Inside is a power-up and 100 Coins.

Upon leaving the Pipe, hop onto the second Column to the right and jump up: there's an Invisible Block with a power-up here. Get onto the rightmost Column and leap onto the Kumo. Get back on the little wall to the left; another Kumo will arrive. Stand there and simply drop down on it. Go to the Ledge above to collect not jut the Coins, but a 1-Up in the fourth Block from the right. Six Elevators await: the first moves from side to side, the second to the upper right, the third to the upper left, the

fourth vertically, and the fifth and sixth horizontally. You can actually avoid the sixth if you wish,
but there are Coins you can only access from that
Elevator—and every one is precious at this level.
Immediately after the Elevators is a Pipe. There
are Coins, as well as multiple Coins in the bottom
Block on the center. Just be careful not to fall on
the Spikes!

When you emerge, you can reach the Ledges
above by uncovering an Invisible Block to the right
of the Pipe. Hop the Ledges to the next Pipe, where
it will be necessary to board the horizontal Elevator below. Make certain that you do so while it's
moving to the right, or you'll die. Hop up from the
Elevator when it passes below and to the right of
the Ledge overhead. Jump from that Ledge to the
top Ledge on the right, then down onto the Elevator
when it's shifting to the right. Jump from the Elevator to the Ledge on the right, then up to the
Ledge on the left, then to the top Ledge. Fall and
go right. When you reach the "altar" of Blocks, a
Batadon will arrive: leap onto the altar when the
flying monster goes left, then jump down onto it. A
Tokotoko is waiting on the other side, but won't
present much difficulty. Vault onto the next altar,
get a power-up from the leftmost ? and Coins from
the two on the right. Just don't get flattened by the
Ganchan, which comes rolling down from the steps
on the right. Leap the Pit and clear the Coins from
the next row—this time, watching out for a Batadon. All you have to do is get on top of the ? row
and jump down on the monster, then clear out the

Coins. Climb the next set of steps and leap the Waterfall. Once you're across, it's time to tango with Hiyoihoi—Tokotoko who flings Ganchans at you. If you're not Super Mario, you've got virtually no chance of getting past the monster. Though there's a Ledge above Hiyoihoi, you can hitch a ride on Ganchan after Ganchan, edging closer each time, and then leap up. (Fortunately, if you die here, you go back to where the power-up was located!) The way to get through is to leap the boulders and shoot the albino with ten Super Balls. If you're Super Mario *and* desperate, you can waste your power-up by taking a hit from a boulder as you literally run through Hiyoihoi,

4/1: Bop the three ?'s for Coins, then go left and go down the Pipe, skewing right as you do so, or you'll miss the Coin Ledge. If you stay above ground, there are Coins in the first three ?'s and a power-up in the Block on the left of the next row. The second inverted Pipe contains a Pakkun Flower nipping down at you; the upward-opening Pipe after it also contains a Pakkun. If you don't have Super Balls, move past the first when it withdraws, wait until the second Pakkun goes down, and move on. (There's nothing in the Blocks overhead here.) You'll find Coins in the next two Blocks, but a Pionpi comes hopping at you from the right. These beings can only be stunned for five seconds by leaping on them; shooting them with two Super Balls is the one way to make sure they stay dead. If you're unarmed, stun the little fellow and move on,

hurrying past the Pakkun Flower to the next two
?'s, which also contain Coins. Keep in mind that
the Pionpi will follow you until you board the Elevators.

Leap off the second Elevator onto the two ?
Blocks, going down and clearing the Coins from
them between shots from the Cannon on the right.
Get onto the Cannon, hopping onto the row of ?'s
and clearing the Coins from them when the Pionpi
is headed left. When you leap the Ledge, you'll be
greeted by another Pionpi and a bomb-toting Turtle:
get the latter before the former arrives. The three
Blocks immediately overhead contain nothing, but
the sole ? on top has multiple Coins. Don't leap the
Pit immediately: wait for a second Pionpi to arrive.
Wait until he's gone to the left, then proceed. Why
did you wait? Because the next Ledge is a duplicate
of this one, except that there are *two* Nokobons to
deal with. If the Pionpi hadn't come over, he would
have been waiting for you there! The Blocks above
you contain nothing; the single ? on top has just
one Coin. Wait and, again, let a Pionpi come over
from beyond the Pit to the right, so that you only
have to deal with one Pionpi when you get there.

Cross the Pit to the Pipes: the third and fourth
contain Pakkuns, and there's a Cannon in the fifth.
Worse, the Pionpi will cross the Pit and come after
you. So, hop the Pipes as soon as the Pakkuns go
down, get on top of the Cannon, and jump to the
last Pipe in that row—it's the tallest one; the Giras
won't hit you up there. Across the Pit there's a Pakkun Flower in the second Pipe and a Pionpi just to

the right of it. Hop onto the Pipe when the Pakkun goes down, kill or stun the Pionpi, scroll him off the screen by hopping onto the first Pipe—he won't return—then double back and clear the Coins from the three ?'s overhead. Hop on the Pakkun Pipe when the Flower goes down, get on the last Pipe, and leap onto the Elevator. The first Elevator moves diagonally to the upper left, the next to the upper right. They're a piece of cake. You'll come to five Pipes in a row: one opening up, two opening down, another up, and the last armed with a Cannon. The first four all contain Pakkuns, so proceed using the stop-and-go technique—making sure that after the third Pipe, you hit the last Block on the overhead Ledge: there are multiple Coins—then jump onto the Cannon Pipe when the weapon is down.

There's a Pakkun in the next downward-opening Pipe; hurry past it when it withdraws and wait. A Chibibo will come by, and you'll want to get rid of it before continuing—taking care that you don't jump up into a Gira from the Cannon. Once the mushroom top is slain, do stop-and-go past the Pakkuns in the Pipe; when you come to an overhead Ledge of breakable Blocks, hit the last Block for a power-up. Once again, stop-and-go past the Pakkun Pipes, the first and fourth of which open up, the middle two opening downward. The last Block on the Ledge overhead contains multiple Coins. (Just watch out for the falling Block, like those you dealt with in 1/3.) When you've cleared the next two Elevators, you'll have to cross a series of breakable Blocks *fast* and then avoid the Cannon in the second Pipe and the Pionpi beyond. Land on the Cannon, bop the little man, and continue right, leaping the next Pionpi and defeating the two Chibibos. (There's a power-up in the lone Block overhead; wait on the Chibibos if you need Super Balls, get them, then blast the little critters.) Leap onto the Elevator on the other side and jump onto the Ledge: you'll fine a power-up in the Block above. A third Elevator will take you to a Ledge; jump from it to the Ledge on the right, then up to the left, to the L-shaped Coin repository above. Be careful, though, when you return to the Ledge on the right after reaping the riches: to the right are *three* Cannons firing at you from three different heights! It'll be necessary to jump from the top of one Cannon to the next, taking care not to step on the Chibibo marching sentrylike after the second Cannon. After you clear the last Cannon, three Pionpis will charge at once on the other side; shoot or bop 'em *fast*. There's a Coin in the ? atop the row of three Blocks, and three more Cannon after that, firing at different heights as before. The only difference is that there's no Chibibo here; deal with them as before. You'll see the Elevator to the right; before you jump onto it, note where the Cannon are firing—they'll have changed direction because you've passed them. Plan your move accordingly, going from the Elevator to the collapsible Blocks and into the room at the top of the Tower.

4/2: Begin by leaping the Ledges over the water; there's no danger until you reach the two ?'s over-

head. There's a Chibibo on the Ledge beneath them.
Poise yourself on the right edge of the Ledge above
the Chibibo and shoot it or drop onto it. Scurry to
the right before it explodes, then go back to the ?'s
and collect the Coins. Repeat this procedure at the
next Chibibo . . . though you'll also have to keep an
eye on the Pompon Flower below. It isn't difficult
to avoid . . . as long as you don't rush ahead. Wait
until the Flower is on the far *left*, then do as before,
with one exception. After you bop the Chibibo, *rush*
to the right and hop onto the row of ?'s. The reason?
A Cannon is firing from the right, and will nail you
if you dally. After the Gira has passed and the Chibibo has exploded, hit the ?'s for power-ups. Leap
up to the Ledge on the right and drop down on the
top of the Cannon. There's a Chibibo to the right,
but that doesn't matter: you're going to go down
the Cannon Pipe, and the Turtle will be gone when
you emerge.

It's vital that you have Super Ball power in the
Pipe, since there are 200 Coins in here and *no*
Blocks. You can clear out half of them without Super Balls—some by from the ground, others by leaping off the top of the exit Pipe—but the weapon is
a *big* help. When you reach the Dragon, hop onto
the Ledge level with it, to the left, and jump up.
This will cause the monster to fire its flame up,
leaving the way clear for you to leap to the right
and bop it on the head. After the Dragon, bust the
Wall with the Chibibo behind it and collect the
goodies up there—all Coins, save for a power-up,
second Block from the left. If you aren't Super, you

must stay below, and you'll find Pakkun Flowers in
all the down-facing Pipes. Go through them using
stop-and-go, but scroll the screen *slowly*: when you
reach the Wall on the right, you're going to hop up
to the left to get some of the goodies on top. When
you go back to the Wall, be ready to leap down fast:
a Cannon to the right is firing at you.

You'll travel through an identical set of Pipes
with Pakkun Flowers—plus the Cannon that was
firing at you—after which you'll reach another series of Ledges: there's a Chibibo on the Ledge to
the upper right, and a Pompon Flower below it.
Leap onto the bottom-center Ledge when you can
leap over the Pompon (this is not difficult) and get
the power-up from the left Block above you. Then
it's time for some fun with a new menace: the
Sparks. These are little fireballs that orbit Blocks
in a counterclockwise direction. (In general: for the
Sparks on the ground, it's safe to stand directly to
either side of the central Block, or on top of it. The
Spark won't touch you here, and you'll definitely
want these havens as you edge your way through.)
Hop over the first Spark, then watch out at the second one, located above: there's a Pakkun Flower in
the Pipe below it. Wait until the Flower is down
and the Spark is moving away, then leap the Pipe
and hug the right side until you can move past the
third Spark. A Chibibo is waiting beyond this one;
kill it, then approach the fourth Spark, which also
has a Chibibo patrolling under it. Wait until the
Turtle has moved to the right before going after it:
kill it, then return to the ? that was the hub of the

fourth Spark. (The Spark will be gone, having been scrolled off the screen to the left.) Bop the ? and get a Star, which should last you through the next Dragon.

After you get the Star, you'll cross a pair of horizontally-shifting Elevators, after which there's another power-up in the ?, which is the hub of the first Spark on this side. There's a second Spark, and another set of horizontally-shifting Elevators; watch when you jump off the second Elevator or you'll hit your head on the overhead Block and fall in the water. Wait until the Elevator is *all the way* to the right before getting off. Also beware the Chibibo waiting for you on the other side. There's an Invisible Block with a Coin directly above the Pipe to the right of the lower Elevator. When you reach the Dragon, deal with it as you did the previous one. You'll pass two more Sparks. Kill the Chibibo on the Ledge above, get down when it explodes— and also to avoid the Spark—continue past the second Spark, and you'll face a third Dragon. After defeating it, run across the widely spaced Blocks using the B button technique, making sure you stop after the last Block so you don't run into the Pakkun Flower in the downward-facing Pipe. When you reach the end of the platform, get to the *very edge* and jump up and slightly to the right when the vertically-moving Elevator is down. If you're not on the edge, you won't be able to get on the lift. Upon getting off at the top, you'll notice there's a breakable Block in the Bridge. Step on it and fall with it, skewing Mario to the right as you do so. If you *don't* shift him to the side, he won't land on solid ground and will perish. If you need more time to study your surroundings as you fall, simply hop up; even though the Block is dropping, it's still solid. Climb to the top of the Tower.

4/3: This level's a lot like 2/3 in terms of strategy: like that round, this one scrolls, inexorably, and you're borne along with the wind. The only difference is that you should play in the middle as soon as the Rocketons start appearing: they not only fire forward, but also backward. You'll want to give yourself some extra maneuvering room to avoid their missiles—which, alas, are immune to your own blasts and also survive the scrolling-off or destruction of the ship.

Very few of the Blocks contain useful objects. There are power-ups in the first and fifth Blocks overhead, and a Star two Blocks later, overhead. Indeed, it's a good idea to play this round entirely in the upper half until you reach the maze: there's virtually nothing of use below. It's easy enough to shoot at the Blocks on top, since you'll be firing in that direction to kill enemies anyway! When you first enter the maze, hang to the left until you clear out the four foes that attack. They can go through Walls—you can't, of course—so beware! Enemies will only appear in the first few corridors of the maze. After they stop attacking, you'll enter a massive Coin room. When you've cleaned it out—you have to do this by touching them: your bullets won't garner them here—drop to the bottom, shoot the

lower right-hand Wall, and continue. Your course
after shattering the Wall will be right, up, right,
down, right, up, right, down, and finally, right.
What's important here is that you stay to the
right, and go up and down vertical corridors as
quickly as possible: the screen will scroll you left
faster than you think! Fortunately, there are no enemies in here to distract you. When you exit, you'll
have to face three Sparks: one alone, at first—
simply stay on the bottom to avoid it—then two, one
atop the other. You can pass the second two, as well,
by staying on the bottom. However, when you roll
into their domain, you'll want to go up: there's a
two-Block wall on top, and the upper Block contains a power-up. You'll definitely want that so you
can take a hit and not perish in the climactic two
showdowns. Get the Coins above you to the right,
then watch out for the enemies lurking in the two
downward-opening Pipes: a pair of massive mailed
Fists. *Don't* delay going through them: if the screen
scrolls too far, you'll be *forced* to the right, and not
necessarily at the best time. Head forward the instant the Fists go back in the very first time.

Once you've passed these, you'll shoot through a
Wall and face the evil Blokinton, boss of this level.
As soon as you've gone through the Wall, stay in
the upper half of the room, firing ahead; you'll get
in a few licks before the cloudlike creature attacks
you. You must hit the Cloud twenty times to destroy it; the task is complicated by the vehicles that
constantly emerge from the Cloud in pairs. Blast
these, and stay directly in front of the puffy thug—

that is, to the left—whenever you can. Go to the right of Blokinton, and above or below it, only when it heads left; if you don't, it'll pin you to the left Wall and kill you. Then, as soon as the Cloud shifts back to the right, get on the left side of it again and continue firing. When Blokinton is history, go to the lower right corner, open fire, and get set to battle Tatanga himself. The villain is nestled inside the "war robot" Pagosu, which rises from the floor and launches projectiles that divide, each piece accelerating and fanning out at you. Though these can be felled by a single shot, they keep you from hitting your main target. Stay in the upper left corner of the screen, moving up and down only slightly to avoid the projectiles while you get in your shots at the big boss. It'll take at least two dozen direct hits on Pagosu's cannons to disable the ship and release Tatanga's captive, Daisy. (And, of course, bring on the credits scroll! Speaking of which—congrats to programmers M. Yamaoto and T. Harada, and director S. Okada, for an absolutely terrific game.)

After you win, press Start and the game will begin again . . . though not exactly as you remembered it! Though all the goodies are in the same place as before, your foes have multiplied rather significantly. For example, you'll find a Fly at the first 1-Up in 1/1, and a Gao—yes, a Gao!—perched atop the first multiple Coin Block. Bunbuns attack right away in 1/2, there are more falling Blocks than before in 1/3 . . . and wherever there was one Gao in that level the first time around, there are now two. A pair of Tamao work with Dragonzamasu at the conclusion of 2/3—though that won't affect your strategy at all—while you'll be greeted by a Cannon in the first Pipe of 3/1 . . . and so on. Fortunately, you get "continues" if you lose at any level the second time around. (The continue mode actually begins in the closing levels of the first game. For instance, if you make it to Blokinton's chamber and lose your last Mario, you'll start level 4/3 again with three continues.)

When you become super proficient at *Super Mario Land*, you'll even be able to execute level select. All you have to do is make your way through the game *twice*. (Are there batteries that last that long?) After you do so, a prompt will ask you to select the round and realm you wish to visit. Make your choice with the control pad.

If you're having trouble with the game, you can earn as many lives as you wish . . . assuming you have time and patience. In level 1/1, after you collect the first Star, continue to where the three rows of Blocks give you eight Coins. When you've collected these, leap off the cliff to the right, losing a Mario. When you return, you'll be right underneath the Block where you got the Star. Repeat this process as often as you like! The Heart will keep replacing the life you lost, while those Coins keep on accumulating, giving you extra Marios. (Just don't take a power-up: Super Mario, sans Super Balls, can't get the Coins nestled in those narrow corridors of the Wall at the end of the level.)

Finally, do the following at the end of world 1/1:

if you get into the top of the Tower, hold down the A button while the time-remaining is being added to your score. *Keep* the button pressed as you shift into the bonus stage. You'll be rewarded with three extra Marios almost every time.

SUPER MARIO BROS.

Objective:

Forget Disneyland: the happiest place in the universe is the Mushroom Kingdom, a land ruled by the benevolent Mushroom King and Princess Toadstool, his delightful daughter (despite her name). Unfortunately, the serenity of the Mushroom Kingdom is shattered by the arrival of King Bowser and his army of evil Turtles known as Koopa Troopas and Koopa Paratroopas. The ensuing war is won by Bowser, who uses magic to transform the conquered Mushroom People into Blocks and Plants. Worse, he imprisons Princess Toadstool—the only one with the power to liberate the tyrant's unwilling subjects. But all is not lost! With your help, bold Mario will attempt to reach the castle in whose dungeon Princess Toadstool is incarcerated, and free her. (If a friend is playing with you, Mario's brother Luigi will join him on his quest.) The journey will take

you through eight different worlds comprised of four
levels each.

Gameplay:

Some of the vilest life forms in the universe make
up Bowser's army, and there are three ways Mario
can beat them: he can jump and land on top of them;
bop them by hitting up under Blocks on which
they're standing; or blast them with fireballs.
(When you jump on a Koopa, its Shell can become
a weapon; if you leap on it again, the Shell will
zoom along the ground in the opposite direction,
cutting down enemies like they were bowling pins.
Just make sure you don't get in the way if the Shell
ricochets, or you'll die!) As Mario makes his way
through the kingdom, he obtains various power-up
items that either materialize in the air or must be
uncovered by shattering Blocks. The Power Booster
Mushroom transforms Mario into Super Mario,
while the Starman makes Mario or Super Mario
invincible for just about a half minute. Fire Flowers, which only Super Mario can obtain (Mario can't
jump high enough to get them), give him fireball
power. All power-ups move to the right when they
arrive or are uncovered, though they change direction upon bumping into something. Blocks come in
four different varieties: Breakable Blocks, Unbreakable Blocks, ? Blocks, and Invisible Blocks.

Mario also obtains Coins as he plays. These pro-
vide him with additional lives when he's collected
enough. Some Blocks contain one Coin, others ten

Coins; these will be noted below in *Strategies*. Beware of Blocks, however, when you're about to do battle: if there's a Block overhead when you try to jump on a foe, you won't have enough room to clear your adversary. As a result, it'll run into you—in which case, kiss one Mario good-bye.

If Mario dies, you don't lose the Coins or points you've amassed. Where your next Mario begins depends upon where the previous one perished. Any enemies you've killed will return exactly as before—but the good news is you can re-collect Coins from Blocks. An important note: when Mario stands on a Block or Ledge, it isn't necessary for both feet to be on solid ground. Indeed, to bop up under certain Blocks, it's often necessary to situate Mario on the surface below so that one foot is standing on air!

In addition to running and leaping, Mario has the ability to crouch and squeeze through narrow passageways, which is accomplished by running (with the B button) and, when you reach the tight corridor, by pressing the controller down.

Points:

The prices on enemies' heads range from 100 to 1000 points. Some characters are worth more points depending upon how they're slain. Buzzy Beetle goes from 100 to 200 points if dispatched by an invincible Mario; a 100-point Koopa Troopa doubles in value when fireballed or hit by invincible Mario; a Koopa Paratroopa is worth 400 points instead of

100 points if you jump on them—which is only fair: it's tougher to get on top of the fly-guys. Ditto the Lakitu, whose point value increases from 200 to 400 if you pounce on them. Points are also awarded simply for busting Blocks in Walls or ceilings, and for collecting Coins and power-ups. Even if you have that particular power, go for the item: you'll still get points for it.

Other ways of earning extra points from destroying enemies are: killing two foes at once (that is, with one jump); hopping from one right onto another (each successive leap doubles the score for your previous victim); using a Koopa Shell to cut down foes (see *Gameplay*, above); and stomping a foe, waiting, allowing it to revive, then rekilling it, each new jump earning you increasingly higher points.

At the end of each level you get points for reaching the Flagpole, but you get far more points if, when you leap, you grab the top.

A more daring way to earn bonus points is to remain on a Balance Elevator until the cable snaps, and *then* leap off as the platform is falling. It takes guts, but the 1000 points are worth the risk!

Speed matters in the game: points are also given for the number of seconds remaining on the timer at the end of each world. The more time there is, the more points you get.

Strategies:

Before entering Pipes at any point in the game, consider where they're going to let you out. For example, take a look at the Blocks you'll miss out on if you enter the first Pipe in 1/1. Although you'll avoid danger, you'll also pass up a slew of important power-ups.

Here's a complete guide to each realm of every world.

1/1: From the beginning of this round to the *second* Pit, you'll face only Goombas. The first ? contains a Coin. There's a power-up and Coin in the next row, and a Coin in the ? above it. (Note: if you go for the power-up before you go for the Coin to its right, don't hit the Coin until the power-up has come down. Otherwise, by butting the Coin Block, you'll cause the power-up to roll to the left, right off the screen!) The first three Pipes can't be entered; the fourth contains Coins. However, if you enter it, you'll emerge just a few short hops from the end of the round, missing out on numerous goodies. It's recommended that you avoid the Pipe. Leaping over it, stand on the sixth Block from the left side of the Pit, jump up and you'll hit an Invisible Block which will give you a 1-Up. (If you decide to go down the Pipe, you can still get this 1-Up; just be careful not to scroll the Pipe off the left side of the screen.) Vault the Pit and get a power-up from the ? in the lower row of Blocks. The upper row consists of Unbreakable Blocks.

Jump the next Pit: in addition to Goombas, you'll

have to deal with Koopa Troopas here, so be prepared. Get a Coin from the ? on the top row, right;
the Block beneath it contains multiple Coins. The
rightmost Block of the next row contains a Starman. Four ?'s follow: the one on top is a power-up,
and the bottom three are all Coins. The next two
?'s you encounter (before the Staircase) are both
Coins. Pass the second Staircase, then the third,
leap the Pit to the fourth, and cross over the Pipe.
(Note: this is the Pipe from which you'll exit if you
entered the other Pipe. While leaping on the
Goomba here, don't forget to get the Coin from the
? in the row overhead.)

1/2: You'll enter a Pipe to begin. Until you pass
the first row of eight Walls, you'll only have to deal
with Goombas. (A cinch; in fact, you can mash the
first two with one jump!) The row of ?'s immediately overhead contain, from the left, a power-up
and then all Coins. When you reach the Block after
the sixth Wall, you'll want to get the multiple Coins
from within. However, before you do so, get on top
of the Wall and jump down, flattening the Goomba
beneath the Block (at this angle, your fireballs will
be ineffective). After the last Wall, there'll be
Goombas and Troopas underfoot. When you reach
the overhead Wall, jump up and break the Blocks
on the left side so you can collect the Coins overhead. But don't leave until you've also hopped up
and down under the Wall on the right side: the last
Block on the top has a Starman inside!
   Facing Goombas and Troopas, you'll reach a se-

ries of blue Walls. Get the Coins ahead. If you prefer to travel along the ceiling, free from danger, you
can do the following: as soon as you reach these
Walls, stand under the right side of the leftmost
Wall and break the three Blocks overhead. Hop onto
the Ledge to the right, jump up and bop the two
Blocks of the Wall overhead, leap left onto the remaining part of the first Wall you pounded, jump
up and shatter the Block overhead, in the ceiling,
and jump through the opening. You won't reap the
Coins below, but you'll get a breather. The ceiling
route will let you off at the first Elevator, discussed
below. If you remained on the ground: when you
come to the next Coin—a single Coin sitting on a
Ledge—get it and also break the Block beside it to
get a power-up. The Wall to the right of this has
multiple Coins in the bottom right Block. Get onto
the Ledge by the Pit and jump onto the Coin Ledge.
At the right side, stand on the last Block and leap
straight up: a 1-Up will sprout. As soon as it does,
break the Block beside the Mushroom, let it drop,
then grab it. Below, you'll be battling only Goombas until after you pass the Elevator—which will
be in a few moments. Enter the first Pipe and collect the Coins; make sure you also bop the Block
two Blocks in from the exit Pipe: there are multiple
Coins here. You'll exit not far from where you entered, and will have missed nothing ... except a
few Goombas!

Leap the two Pits, battle the Goombas, and wait
when you reach the Staircase: let the Goombas descend and crunch them before climbing. Cross us-

ing the Elevator, then position yourself under the right side of the overhead Ledge: the last Block contains a power-up. Board the second Elevator, hop off onto the upper Ledge—actually, take a mighty leap right off the screen!—and walk along the roof to the Warp Zone. (If you missed the upper Ledge, jump to the left, back onto an Elevator, and try again. The only time this *won't* work is if you leapt too far right when you got off the Elevator, in which case it will have scrolled off the screen.) The Warp Zone consists of three Pipes which, from the left, will warp you to four, three, and two, respectively. If you want to fight your way through the game, get off the elevator and enter the Pipe. When you emerge, you'll be at the end of 1/2.

1/3: Leap the two Pits to the Mushroom, getting the Coins on top. (Note: the Troopa on top won't come down, so you can deal with it when you ascend.) When you leap to the next Mushroom, the Goombas *will* come after you, so bop them as you go. When you reach the high Mushroom overlooking the floating Coins, get the Coins as you leap to the next Mushroom, board the Elevator, hop onto the high Mushroom with the Coins, then drop down and hit the ? for a power-up. Hop to the next Mushroom, and then prepare to do battle with the Paratroopas! These airborne Turtles can rise *and* fall, so leap on top of them *quickly* to destroy them as you hop from Mushroom to Mushroom. There are Coins above the two horizontally-shifting Elevators, which you can nab as you slide by. Go from the narrow Plateau to the larger one, watching out for both Troopas and Paratroopas there and on the next Mushroom (the one covered with floating Coins). Two more Mushrooms and a single horizontally-shifting Elevator complete the level.

1/4: This is the level where you first meet the rotating Fire Bars. These little delights spin in different directions, and will sizzle you with their touch. You encounter one of these within moments after beginning the round. It moves in a counterclockwise direction, and you should jump over it when it's between the ten and nine on the clock. Leap it, then hit the ? for a power-up, vault to the right to catch the booster if you're Mario, or get on top of the Block to get it if you're Super Mario. The next three Fire Bars come one after the other, all moving in the same direction as the last one. Scoot under the first when it passes the three position, stop and wait for the second to do so, then wait for the third. You can actually take all three at once, if you time it right. Be careful, though: after the third is another Fire Bar moving in a *clockwise* direction. If that fourth one isn't in a favorable position, don't pass through the third until it is. Two more Fire Bars await side by side, the first moving counterclockwise, the second clockwise. Ideally, you should wait until the first is upright and the second pointed straight down; you can jump over the first and run under the second.

You'll be facing the boss of the level shortly, but the monster's presence will already be felt due to

its flaming breath. Make your way forward with
care. When you come to a drop in the floor, step
down: there are a half-dozen Invisible Blocks, each
of which contains a Coin. Jump when you've walked
a few steps, then get on top and take a powerful
one-foot-off-the-Block leap to the right to reach the
next (hopping fireballs as you do). Go down, take a
few steps, jump up, uncover the low Block, get on
it, and repeat. Do this for the next Blocks as well.
After getting the six Coins, shoot Bowser with fireballs. If you don't have any, you can wait until he
shifts positions and leap over him or rush under
him. In either case, you must get to the Axe on the
other side. Use it to cut down the Bridge, and this
demon is history. If you're Super Mario, you can
also run *through* the fiend. It'll cost you your Super
status, but during the few seconds it takes for you
to change from Super Mario to Mario, at least
you're invincible and will be able to get the Axe.
(Note: this Bowser, like the ones you'll be fighting
at the end of each level, isn't really the master
Bowser, but an imposter—a Goomba, to be precise.
You can only reveal the phony's true identity by
killing it with a fireball. For the record, the successive false Bowsers are a Troopa, Buzzy, Spiny, Lakitu, Blooper, and the Hammer Brothers. The last
Bowser you face is the genuine article!)

2/1: Until the Staircase, you'll only face Goombas.
Passing under the row of unmarked Blocks overhead, break the one in the middle: it contains a
power-up. There are Troopas after the Staircase, but

you'll want to stay in their lair just a bit because
of the row of Blocks overhead. Jump to get a Coin
from the Invisible Block to the left of the row. Leap
onto that Block and jump up to reveal another Invisible Block: this one will give you a 1-Up. Nothing much lies ahead—except Goombas and
Troopas—until you pass the next Pipe. The ten ?'s
overhead contain Coins, save for the Block on the
lower left, which will give you a power-up. Continue until you reach a single Block, then get on
top of it, stand with one foot over the right edge,
and leap up to the right, under the leftmost Block,
butting it to reveal a Starman. Invincible, proceed
over the Pipe to the two rows of ?'s, all of which
contain Coins. Now, instead of leaving the ?'s, remain on top and position yourself at the right edge
of the row on the left. Jump up against the Blocks
overhead and you'll cause a Beanstalk to sprout.
Climb it for the Sky Bonus, which consists of rows
of floating Coins that you can only reach by hopping on a Cloud Elevator. It moves horizontally
along the length of the Coins, allowing you to hop
and grab them as it moves to the right. If you happen to fall off, you'll miss a few Coins—but you can
salvage the trip by running to the right, ahead of
the Elevator, and jumping back on. When you're
finished here, just fall off and you'll land near the
end of the realm.

If you stayed on the ground, there's danger . . .
but riches as well. After leaping the Pit and landing on a Goomba Ledge, hop into the Pipe and collect the Coins therein. When you emerge, climb to

the top of the second Pipe you encounter: the left-most Block contains a power-up. After the next Pipe, you'll encounter Troopas and, on the other side of the Pit, Paratroopas. Upon jumping the next Pit and hopping off the wall, you'll battle Paratroopas *and* Goombas; the Ledge overhead (not the Block to the left of it—which, not so incidentally, contains multiple Coins) is the one on which you'll land if you took the Sky Bonus route. The ? to the right has a Coin, the Block to the upper right of it contains a power-up. The latter one's really tough to get if you're Super Mario: you're just too big to fit easily. The best way to bump the Block is to start running while you're under the row of Blocks where you alighted after your sky journey. Jump onto the ? without breaking your stride, then jump again and hit the Block. Your timing must be precise, or you won't pull it off. There are Troopas on the other side of the Pipe, and they'll make it tough to get to the Springboard. However, that little trampoline isn't the only way to get to the top of the Wall on the right. Leap onto the row of Blocks overhead, then hop up and uncover an Invisible Block with a Coin. Get on top of that and you'll be able to vault the Wall. You've made it to the end of 2/1.

2/2: This is an underwater world, complete with Coral to snag you, Whirlpools to drag you down, and new live foes. Your fireballs work just fine here, though, and that's good: they're the only thing that will stop your first foes, the Bloopers. Even better, the Bloopers don't go all the way down to the sea bottom, which means that Mario is completely safe strolling along down there, and Super Mario only needs to duck to avoid them. Nothing much happens apart from run-ins with Coral and Bloopers until you reach the first Pit. There are Coins floating above, and a Whirlpool below; to cross, hold down the A button—using Turbo, if you have the NES Advantage—and pump the button like mad! After swimming through the break in the Wall on the other side of the Whirlpool, you'll be attacked by both Bloopers and Cheep-Cheeps; the latter, like their comrades, must be fireballed to be stopped. When you reach the next Pit, watch out for the Whirlpool and also for the Blocks overhead: if you bang into these, you may get bounced down into the suction. After this Pit, you have only Cheep-Cheeps to worry about through the end of the level. You'll encounter a third Pit moments after the second; it's more challenging than the two that came before, because of the lips that partly cover both sides. If you go down to get the Coins, the exit is much narrower, requiring great navigational skills! There's nothing to obtain, and just the Cheep-Cheeps to avoid, between this point and the Exit Pipe.

2/3: A new form of Cheep-Cheep welcomes you to this Bridge level: the Flying Cheep-Cheep. While fireballs are, again, the best weapons to use against these creatures, they can also be stomped if you're agile enough to get on top of them! You'll find nothing but floating Coins and the Flying Cheep-Cheeps

as you cross the first five Bridges. The sixth Bridge
offers a power-up inside the ?, after which there's
naught but Coins and the airborne fish for the rest
of your journey here. Watch out for the short
Bridges at the end: it's easy for a novice to over-
shoot these and plunge into the void below.

2/4: The living fireballs, Podoboos, make their debut on this level. Fortunately, you don't have to
decide whether to duck the goons or fight: they're
indestructible, so your only option is to hop them
when they appear, do your business in that area,
and get out as soon as possible! They begin appearing as soon as you leap onto the first Ledge you
encounter. While avoiding the Podoboos, jump to
the Ledge on the upper right, go to the right side
of that Ledge and hit the ? overhead for a power-
up. Jump from this Ledge to the next one on the
right, and prepare to pick your way past the Fire
Bars. These are rotating in a counterclockwise direction, so leap the first one when it's pointing to
the imaginary nine o'clock, wait for the next (overhead) to hit three, cross the third and fourth ones
at nine, then wait until the fifth one (overhead) is
a three. There are Elevators beyond this one, the
first set heading up, the second traveling down . . .
and a Fire Arm waiting for you on the other side
(bottom). Time your jumps so that you get off the
last Elevator when the Fire Arm is at the ten position. Also, before you jump on the first Elevator,
make sure you're standing exactly at the edge of
the right side of the platform—the one with the fifth

Fire Arm overhead. If you're too far to the left, you'll hit your head on the Fire Arm Block when you make your jump and plummet into the Elevator shaft.

As soon as you've gotten off the Elevators and cleared the last Fire Arm, the fake Bowser's fire will start rolling in your direction. Avoid it while you collect the floating Coins up ahead, crouching to get your Super Mario under the Block so he can claim the Coins on the bottom. This time, if you don't have Fireballs, Koopa's going to give you a little more trouble than before: there's a Ledge in front of him, which means you have to exercise more caution when leaping the fiend. Again, do this when he moves, get the Axe, and chop down the Bridge.

3/1: The two Paratroopas who attack at the very beginning are easy enough to slay. Do so, then get a Coin, Coin, and power-up, respectively, from the three ?'s overhead. The second Pipe you encounter leads to a a Coin room—obviously, don't jump on top of the Pipe until the Piranha Flower goes down. Inside, you must do the following in this order: stand under the overhead Wall on the left, jump up, and shatter the two lowest Blocks of the Wall. Hop up to the single Block on the right and nab the Coin there; you can probably grab the Coin to the right as well. If you didn't, go down and break the Block it's sitting on, then hop back onto the Block where you got the first Coin. Jump up and shatter the two Blocks directly over you. Take a powerful diagonal leap to the upper right, and break the Block for a power-up. Clear out the remainder of the Coins, working the right side of the room any way you wish.

When you emerge from the Pipe, you'll cross a Bridge where you'll be greeted by a trio of Goombas. Blast or stop them, then go to the right side of the Bridge: if you're Super Mario—and only *sometimes* if you're Mario—jump up and uncover an Invisible Block with a 1-Up inside. Be quick about getting it, though, since it rolls to the right in a hurry. Jump the Pit, stand on the bottom step, and hop up against the Ledge overhead: the leftmost Block will give you a Starman. Rush through the Goombas and Troopas, leap the Pipe, and do battle with the Hammer Brothers. You'll be able to blast the first one easily enough, but the second Hammer-tossing Turtle will hop to the upper levels of the two Ledges ahead. Either bop him off—tough, given the continual rain of Hammers—or hang to the left, wait until he comes back down, and fireball him. Get the Coin and power-up from the left and right ?'s in the upper row.

Now, go back down to the ground, run hard, and jump up to the lower Ledge of the two Ledges ahead, *avoiding* the Springboard. The trampoline will get you to the upper Ledge, but that isn't what you want. Sandwiched between the two Ledges, jump up under the Block on the right and you'll cause a Beanstalk to grow. Climb it to the Sky Bonus and reap the Coins as you did before. If you can't manage to get up there, use the Springboard to get to the top Ledge, hop right to the Staircase, dispatch the Goombas, and climb. When you leap from the Staircase to the other side of the Pit, you'll have to fight Troopas, Paratroopas, and Goombas. Between bouts, get a pair of Coins from the two ?'s in the Ledges on the left, a Coin from the upper Ledge on the right, and a power-up from the lower Ledge on the right. The Ledge you come to is the one on which you'll land when you drop from the Sky Bonus. The second Block from the left on this Ledge contains multiple Coins. Leap the Wall, jump over the Pit, climb the Stairs—you'll be fighting Troopas here—and you've made it.

3/2: The enemy population is heavy here, with Troopas and Goombas both; it's advisable to kick the Shells of dead Troopas to make headway. You won't encounter any Blocks for a while; the first appears after the floating Coins, and it contains a power-up. Afterward, there are plenty more Troopas and Goombas to occupy you. When you reach the low Walls with a pair of Blocks floating between them, up above, leap from the left Wall to the top Block, get the Starman in there, then go for the multiple Coins in the lower Block. If you try to do it the other way around, Troopas will feast on your bones!

After you jump the Pit beyond the right Wall, you'll find no rewards: just Troopas, Paratroopas, and Goombas. Deal with them as you did at the beginning of the round. Leap the next Pit and carefully jump the Wall; if you jump too high, the Block on top will knock you into the Pit to the right. (The Block, by the way, is empty.) Troopas only will dog your steps until you reach the floating Coins, after which they'll be joined by Goombas. Climb the Staircase, jump down, and you're ready for—

3/3: Leap onto the first Mushroom and wait there until the Goombas drop from the second Mushroom; jump up and crush them. There are two horizontally-shifting Elevators: ride the first to the second, and jump either to the Coins floating above the Mushroom, or to the Mushroom to the right of it, and just hop down. Jump to the Mushroom on the right, get the floating Coins, then obtain a power-up from the ? on top of the next Mushroom— watching out that the many Troopas here don't nail you. Get the Coins on the lower right, then jump up to the ? again and leap to the high Mushroom on the right. Get the Coins there, then board the Elevator to the right . . . keeping in mind that as soon as Mario steps on it, the lift will fall like a wingless Paratroopa! Leave it quickly—taking care to land on the high, thin Mushroom to the right. If you land on the ground, you're sunk: there's no way off.

After collecting the Coins on top of each Mushroom, jump onto the highest one and go from there to the Balance Elevator. Like the scales of justice, these tip one way when Mario is on them. Get on the left side, hop onto the Mushroom between the Elevators, then jump to the one on the right. Leave this one as it falls, jumping onto one of the two

Elevators shifting horizontally to the right—one of these two is high, the other low; get on whichever is nearest. Hop to the thin Mushroom to the right, get onto the horizontally-shifting Elevator beside it, and collect the floating Coins from the three closely-set Mushrooms. Watch out for Paratroopas, which arrive as you prepare to hop the Pit to the next Mushroom; fireball them before you jump, or else bop them with extreme caution. Go from the thin Mushroom to the wide one, which is covered with Troopas; get onto the horizontally-shifting Elevator to the right; cross another Balance Elevator, and you've won the level.

3/4: This one's a toughie. Not only are there Fire Bars spinning counterclockwise over the Pits you have to jump, but those same Pits are disgorging Podoboos. There are four Pits to clear, guarded by three Fire Bars; leap each bar sometime after it's passed the ten position *and* when there are no Podoboos gushing out. (At least there are no walking, leaping, or flying monsters here!) You'll come to a Ledge of ?'s: from the left, you'll find a Coin, power-up, and Coin in them. To the right, you'll find something a whole lot more unpleasant: three pairs of Fire Bars. The first two on top are moving counterclockwise, the bottom two clockwise. The last set is going clockwise on top, counterclockwise on the bottom. The only way to make it through is to watch the movements of each pair of arms, leap between them when there's room, stop, and examine the next set before proceeding. The key is to keep your

eye on the top Fire Bar: if you jump high enough,
you can leap the bottom one when it's at most any
position. Just make sure you've got the room on top
before you do so—that is, be certain the Fire Bar
up there is out of the way. Another quartet of Pits
lies ahead: no Fire Bars this time, only a steady
stream of Podoboos as well as the fire from the mock
Bowser at the end of the level. All you can do is
jump with care and precision. When you face the
sham Bowser, it's going to be tough getting over
him because of how *close* he is to the Wall that
blocks the Elevator. If you don't have fireballs,
you'll need to be super skillful to avoid his blasts,
get over him, and grab the Axe.

4/1: You're about to meet one of the game's most
taxing foes: a Lakitu, which slides back and forth
overhead, following you wherever you go and constantly dropping Spinys at you. When the Spinys
hit the ground, these horned Turtles shift back and
forth trying to kill you. To begin the round, hop the
Pipe to the right—when the Piranha Flower goes
down, that is—and you'll see two ?'s, one atop the
other. The Lakitu will appear as soon as you've
reached these. Get the lower one first: it's a power-
up, and you may need it. Grab the Coin from the ?
on top, then *hurry* ahead, leaping the Pit and not
breaking stride as you jump to grab the floating
Coins above. The Lakitu will be ahead of you; while
running, fireball any Spinys that get in your way—
you can't step on them, or you'll die. Upon reaching
the set of four ?'s in the sky, don't bop them . . . not

yet, anyway. Leap onto the lower left ? and position yourself on the right edge, with one foot off the Block, in midair. (Do this quickly: the Lakitu can drop Spinys right on the Blocks themselves!) Jump from there to the top right ? This will put you at the same height as the Lakitu. When it slides in your direction, hop up and bop it on the head to slay it. Take care not to miss, and especially not to fall off: there'll be so many Spinys around, it'll be tough not to land on one *or* get back onto the ? Block. Now you can clear out the ?'s at your leisure, all of them Coins.

After jumping the Pit, raid the Ledge of ?'s for Coins, then get on top of the Ledge, stand on the second ? from the right, jump up against the Invisible Block, and get yourself a 1-Up. Continue to the right, hopping onto the wall and leaping from it to get the floating Coins. Do the same thing when you reach the Pipe a short distance beyond it. No Lakitu will bother you during this stretch. Enter the next Pipe if you wish to avoid the monster's return; in addition to the Coins, there's a power-up in the Block atop the exit Pipe, though it's virtually impossible for Super Mario to fit under there. If you stayed aboveground, the Lakitu returns as soon as you jump over the treasure-chamber access Pipe. Run and grab the floating Coins, get on top of the two tiers of ?'s, and again crown the Lakitu when it floats by. All of the ?'s contain Coins, save for the third Block from the left on the bottom row, which has a power-up. The Blocks directly over the Pit contain nothing.

Leap the next Pipe—this is where you would've emerged if you'd entered the Coin room—blasting any Spinys in your way as you leap the two Pits and hop onto the Wall ahead. There, you can try and battle the Lakitu as before. This is also a good vantage point from which to launch fireballs at the creature. Cross the Pit, climb the Staircase, and jump down. The Block to the left of the Flagpole contains multiple Coins, so go down and collect them. When you're through, climb onto the Block and jump back onto the top of the Staircase. This will enable you to take a stab at reaching the top of the Flagpole.

4/2: Don't breathe a sigh of joy because you've left the Lakitus behind. The Goombas will more than keep your hands full on this level, as will the Buzzy Beetles, which are impervious to fireballs. They can only be slain by getting squashed, hit by an Invincible Mario, or bopped off a Block by hitting it from below.

After entering the Pipe at the beginning of the round, leap the three Pits, then hop to the top of the Ledge in front of you. Slip down the vertical passageway at the end, collect the Coins, and jump up to break the Block on the far right of the lip overhead. You'll receive a power-up. Jump up into the corridor on the right, but take care: Goombas patrol here, and it's too narrow to do any serious bopping. Thus, as you proceed, smash the overhead Blocks to give yourself room. (You'll also give yourself one thing more. No, not a headache: the fifth

Block from the right contains multiple Coins!) When you emerge from the narrow passageway, you'll find three rows of ?'s: all contain Coins, except for the second ? from the right in the rightmost row, which will give you a power-up. Board the Elevator to the right and get off before it sinks. Stop where you are and pay attention: this is truly a magical area!

Position yourself under the right end of the Ledge and jump up. You'll reveal an Invisible Block and collect a Coin. Move slightly to the left and jump up again to uncover a second Invisible Block and a Coin. Go left again, jump up and bop a third Invisible Block and Coin, then repeat a fourth time. Return to the first Block you uncovered, jump on top, then climb onto the second and third Blocks. Hit the Block overhead to cause a Beanstalk to sprout, then use the last Block you exposed to get up to the vine. When you reach the Sky Bonus, clear away the Coins and climb the Staircase. On the other side is a Warp Zone, Pipes that you can use to fast-forward yourself to Worlds Six, Seven, or Eight.

If you're slightly demented (like us!) and want to struggle through the intervening worlds, forget about the Sky Bonus and continue through 4/2. You'll come to a series of Pipes. There's a Troopa after the first. Kill it, get on the Ledge, and jump just to the left of the second Pipe to obtain multiple Coins. A Buzzy follows the second Pipe. Slay it and leap up, just to the right of the second Pipe, to reveal a Starman. The third Pipe contains a Coin room, and the only reason not to enter is if you need a power-up or want to Warp to World Five. If you do, stay on the surface. You'll battle a Buzzy after the third Pipe, and Troopas after the fourth. There's a Wall, a Pipe, and another Wall, all of which must be hopped, after which you'll reach a downward-moving Elevator. The power-up is located in the middle Block of the second Ledge. Collect it, board the upward-moving Elevator, and get onto the ceiling on the right. Follow it—endlessly, it will seem!—leaping a second Elevator and ultimately reaching the Warp Zone.

If you're still determined to stay on the ground, get off that upward-moving Elevator at the Pipe Ledge—this is also where the Coin room will let you out. Deal with the Troopas beyond, then hop the next two Pipes and a Pit, climb the Staircase, leap onto the downward-moving Elevator when it's at the top, then get off *at once* onto the Coin Ledge. If you fail at this and can't get up there, take some consolation in the power-up you'll find in the left-most Block of the Coin Ledge. Climb the Staircase to the right: there's a Pipe to the right, and a Buzzy at its base. Edge to the right of the step and jump with caution. When you land on the Pipe, don't try to get to the Exit Pipe with one jump: the chances are good you'll hit the ceiling and drop into the Pit below. Instead, slide off the Pipe and land on its right base, jump up to the Ledge on which the Exit Pipe is sitting, and stroll in. Climb the Staircase, jump to the Flagpole, and gird yourself for a level that demands precision leaping! Take heart, though: you're halfway through the videogame!

4/3: The new twist here is that the Paratroopas
fly up as well as down. At least they don't home in
on you, making them easy enough to duck. Hop onto
the first Mushroom, skip the super-high second
Mushroom for the moment and go to the third—
fireballing or stomping the Troopas there—*then*
double back to the second. Go back to the third, get
a running start, and take a mighty leap onto the
fourth Mushroom—carefully avoiding those versatile Paratroopas here. Skip the short Mushroom
below and go to the one beyond it, claiming the
power-up from the ?. Then drop off to the left, to the
lower Mushroom, get the floating Coins, and jump
to the Mushroom to the right. To get the floating
Coin beyond it, hop on the Balance Elevator and
sweep it up when you sink. Don't try jumping for
the Coin and returning to the Mushroom; you'll fall
to your death.

Leap from the Elevator to the Mushroom and onto
the other side of the Balance Elevator, grabbing
the floating Coin while it sinks. Hop onto the
vertically-moving Elevator beyond, and then, if
possible, onto the one after that when it's ascend-
ing; that's the best way to get onto the floating
Coins Mushroom on the right. (Besides, there are
Troopas on the Mushroom below it, and you might
not want to bother with them.) Hop to the Coin
Mushroom to the right, fireball or stomp the Troopas
on the Coinless Mushroom, then drop to it and
destroy the Troopas on the Mushroom between
them. Get the Coin, hop back up to the right, and

cross the series of three Balance Elevators. One
fairly obvious rule applies to all of the Elevators:
don't try to go from the left to the right side when
the latter is higher than the one you're on. Moreover, if you miss this jump-off window, don't risk a
super leap. There are Mushrooms in the center of
each set of Elevators; use these as stepping-stones
to the other side, if necessary. Upon clearing the
last one, you'll be on a Mushroom covered with
floating Coins. No foes will bother you as you hop
across the remaining Mushrooms to the last Elevator. To reach the top of the Flagpole from this
vertically-shifting platform, wait until it reaches
the top, press the B button for speed, and jump.

4/4: There are no live foes until the very end of this
section . . . but don't imagine that things are going
to be easy here. (You *didn't* think that, did you?)
As you bound down the steps and hop the two Pits,
you'll notice that there are two routes you can take:
upper and lower. Take the upper; the lower route
is a dead-end from which there's no getting out. As
you set out across the top, you'll encounter six Pits
with incredibly narrow plateaus between them.
Press the B button and run over these; if you fall,
you'll end up in the dead-end section below. When
you reach the large Pit at the end of this section,
leap over and land on the bottom portion of the broken Wall ahead. Go from this to the floor ahead,
then leap up the three successive Ledges to the
top. When you come to the first Pit, drop down, go
left, then drop down the Pit you'll find there. Head

right on the bottom level. If you take any other route, you'll be dead-ended!

Travel along the bottom, watching out for the one Fire Arm turning clockwise as you go. At the end of this passageway, jump up onto the Wall, and duck into the Pit beyond to avoid the imposter Bowser's fire. See the Fire Arm right before the monster? It's turning clockwise. You're going to have to wait until the Fire Arm is between the three and eight positions, leap over the alien, and get the Axe. When you do, you'll have completed the fourth world.

5/1: A long, flat stretch full of Goombas and Troopas welcomes you to this new world; kick the Shells for extra points. Hop the first Pipe, the Pit Beyond, and the second Pipe, then cross the next plain, battling Goombas and Paratroopas. When you reach the Wall shaped like a lopsided L, hop on top and break the second Block of the Ledge above it. You'll get a much-needed Starman. While you're invincible, leap the Pit, trample the Goombas, and charge the Turtle Cannon, which is firing Bullet Bills. Since you're invincible, you can run right through 'em all! (In any case, if you step right up to a Turtle Cannon, it won't fire.) After clearing the Cannon, vault the Pit to the Wall on the other side. The field beyond is populated by Goombas and Troopas, after which there's a Wall with a Ledge to the right of it. If you've gotten to this point *without* being hit, you'll find a 1-Up on the right side of the Wall, below the level of the Ledge.

Leap the Pit, watching out for Paratroopas and the Bullet Bills fired by a Turtle Cannon to the right, then get on the Cannon and jump to the Pipe to the left. Enter the Coin room and clean it out thusly: get on the Block over the Exit Pipe, leap to the Ledge on the left, hop up to the top of the Coin chamber, cross and jump onto the left Wall, and drop from there, diagonally, into the Coin chamber. After collecting the wealth, get multiple Coins from the Block over the Exit Pipe—Super Mario will have a very tough time doing that. When you emerge, the Turtle Cannon will be to your rear and there'll be another to your right. Scroll the left Cannon off the screen as quickly as possible, and get on top of the other Cannon to scope out the Paratroopas here—then beat the wings off them as you hop to the nearby Staircase. Jump from the top step to the nearby Wall to the Flagpole to end the round.

5/2: Things really start to heat up with this realm, which is easily the toughest one yet! Mount the Staircase with caution: there's a Turtle Cannon on top. Ascend between shots and get on top of the Cannon to proceed. See if you can get the Floating Coins with a leap from the Cannon; if not, pick your way through the Troopas on the ground and use the Springboard up ahead—again, timing your springs to avoid the Bullet Bills. The Springboard will also prove useful getting you to the Coin Ledge to the right. In addition to the money, the rightmost Block of the top Ledge contains a power-up. Watching out for Paratroopas, go to the Staircase to your immediate right. You'll have to deal with the Hammer Brothers before you can ascend; this is tricky because they momentarily merge from time to time at the top of the Staircase, making them invulnerable. If you haven't got fireball power, you're going to have to jump on them between axe throws. No fun, that!

The pipe after the Staircase leads to an underwater world, which it's recommended that you *avoid*. There are too many goodies on and over the ground to obtain, especially in the Sky Bonus. If you *do* submerge yourself, you'll face Bloopers for most of your swim, and Cheep-Cheeps at the very end. The twist down here is that there are Elevators over two of the Whirlpools; if you don't make your crossing fast enough, the Elevators will push you down. If you remained on the land—

There are Goombas between the Pipe and the next Staircase, which is just a few hops away. Leap from the top step to the Wall on the other side of the Pit, then proceed slowly: the Hammer Brothers stand guard at the bottom. After disposing of them, collect Coins from each of the ?'s in the Ledge overhead. When you've done this, jump to the next Ledge, collect the Coins, then drop off on the *left* side. When you're on the ground, leap up next to the right side of the Ledge to reveal an Invisible Block with a Coin. Climb the Block, and jump up against the left side of the Ledge overhead. This will cause a Beanstalk to sprout. Climb it for a Sky Bonus, and clear it out as you did the first one in the game (2/1). When you're finished with this, you'll land well ahead of many dangers! If you remained on the ground—

Leap the Pit to the right, aware that a Turtle Cannon will be shooting at you from the other side, and that Paratroopas will be falling. After clearing the Cannon, get on the Pipe—this is the Exit Pipe from which you'll emerge if you took the underwater route. You'll have to fight both the Hammer Brothers and Buzzy Beetles here, so watch out! The best tack is to jump on the lower Ledge to the right and butt the rightmost Block on top. Catch the Starman as it emerges, taking care not to fall down the Pit as you do so. Hop the Pit to the Wall, where you'll be dealing with Bloopers and Cheep-Cheeps—obviously, refugees from the underwater world! The first Ledge you encounter has multiple Coins in the Block on the left and a power-up in the one on the right. (This is where you'll come down after your foray into the Sky Bonus.) Get on top of this Ledge and vault the Pit to the Ledge on the right, then take your pick: go up to the Ledge to battle Troopas, or descend and fight Goombas and Paratroopas on the ground. In any case, head to the Block before the next Pit and gather the power-up. Use that Block as a stepping-stone to the Coin Ledge on the right, then look out before continuing to the next plateau: Paratroopas await. Clear the next two Pits and you're home-free!

5/3: This level introduces the new, lethally-improved Bullet Bills, which cover the *entire* game field! Be ready to get out of the way at a moment's notice. Hop to the first Mushroom and then to the second two-tiered Mushroom, stomping the Troopas into oblivion and gathering the Coins. There are Goombas on the next three Mushrooms, so be careful as you jump down to the skinny Mushroom on the right, then up to the next Mushroom and on to the one beyond that. Turn and jump left to get the Coins, landing on the Mushroom below. Go back to the high Mushroom and take a long jump down to the Mushroom to the right, catching the floating Coins as you do so. Use the vertically-moving Elevator to hop onto the Coin-laden top of the Mushroom, then *carefully* drop down to the ? at the left edge of the Mushroom below, get under it, and obtain the power-up. The next two Mushrooms are free of foes, but the third is protected by Goombas and Paratroopas. You have to build up a good head of steam on the first and second Mushrooms to leap the gaping Pit to the third; just make sure you don't hit any Paratroopas on the way over. If you want, try using the Turtles as mini-Ledges, actually bouncing off their Shells as you cross the chasm!

There are two horizontally-shifting Elevators to the right. When they pass under the floating Coins overhead, deftly leap up and grab them. Collect the Coins floating over the next Mushroom, then wait and have a look at what the Troopas are doing on the Mushroom to the right. Jump over there when you can and leap down to the following Mushroom, collecting the Coins and killing the Paratroopas that descend. The next two Mushrooms are devoid of enemies—except for the ever-present Bullet Bill—

and if you can leap onto the vertically-moving Elevator to the right, you can avoid the Troopas on the ground. Hop from the Elevator to the Staircase, hurl yourself from the pinnacle, and get the Flagpole!

5/4: Just what you needed: more Fire Arms! And to start with, the first one you must face is nearly half as long as the standard Bowser-issue Fire Arm. Worse, the Pit beneath it contains Podoboos. So, leap onto the small Ledge to the left of the Fire Arm when the clockwise-moving flames are at the ten o'clock position and there are no fireballs spewing from below. Get onto the Fire Arm Ledge as soon as it swings past one o'clock. Bop the ? overhead *fast* and collect the power-up. If you aren't quick enough and the Fire Arm is headed your way, you can leap onto the ? for sanctuary and take a short hop up when the flames come around. Get onto the Ledge to the right of the Fire Arm, and hurry to the Wall just beyond it. There are an upper and lower corridor ahead: both take you to the same place, but there are fewer Fire Arms sweeping across the top corridor. Naturally, you're going to have to edge your way through the passageway. So you'll know, the first Fire Arm—which touches only the bottom—moves clockwise, the second (both) moves counterclockwise, the third (bottom) rotates clockwise, and the fourth (top), fifth (both), sixth (bottom), and seventh (middle), all move counterclockwise. Once you've gotten by these, there's one more counterclockwise-moving Fire Arm to avoid when you leap onto the Wall. Go past it when it's at the two o'clock position.

Two Elevators await, the one on the left moving up, the other going down. They're easy enough to cross, though you can't dilly-dally since you've got the Fire Arm behind you and another one—turning clockwise—on the wall ahead of you. When you jump to the Wall ahead, go to the right edge and wait: the Fire Arm behind you can't reach, and you'll want to have a look at the Pit beyond before continuing. There's a clockwise-moving Fire Arm in the center, with Coins above and below it. Wait until the Fire Arm is facing straight down, then jump across and grab the Coins on top. As the Fire Arm swings around, scoot to the left and collect the Coins on the bottom. Wait in the left-hand corner and, when the flames are once again pointing in the six o'clock position, hop over the Block in the center and jump onto the Wall on the right. Piece of cake. (Sure!) P.S.: while you're engaged in this undertaking, you have to watch out for Bowser's fire, which will begin coming at you the instant you get off the second Elevator. If you get sizzled by it, your derring-do will leave you looking like a derring-doughnut!

You're poised, now, on the Wall after clearing the Fire Arm. There are two Pits beyond, each with Podoboos. What's more, there are also Podoboos in the Pit beneath the pseudo-Bowser ahead. You're going to do a bit more stopping-and-going as you proceed, due to the little fire fellows; otherwise, it's business as usual to beat Bowser.

6/1: The super-pesky Lakitu returns this round, the only foe you'll have, beginning immediately after you clear out the first two ?'s—a pair of Coins—and jump the Pit. Climb the Staircase quickly to get high enough to stomp the critter . . . going all the way to the small Ledge at the top of the screen, if necessary. When the airborne pest is gone, get under that upper Ledge and hit the Block on the left for a power-up. Descend to the Ledge on the right and bump up under the Block on the right for multiple Coins. Drop to the ground and race ahead, leaping the Pit, grabbing the floating Coins, and hurrying up the Staircase—again, to stay on top of your foe. Jump over the Pit, again scooping up the floating Coins as you go. Hop onto the inverted L-shaped Ledge, and vault from there to the tall Staircase beside it. Use this vantage point to deal with yet more of the dogged Spiny-spawning foes, then drop to the *lowest* of the two Ledges on the right. Jump up: if you haven't been hit to this point, you'll be rewarded with a 1-Up. If you *have* been hurt . . . well, just try to be more careful next time!

Jump over the Pit and make your way onto the nearby Pipe as quickly as possible; one guess why. Lakitu attack! If you can't get the fiend from up here, leap to the right—grabbing the Coins as you go—and hurry to the Staircase. If you have time, jump up just before you get on the Staircase, to uncover an Invisible Block with a Coin. If you still haven't slain the Lakitu, do so from the top of the Staircase, then step onto the Ledge, jump to the row of ?'s to the right, and drop to the Ledge below. You'll get a power-up from the left ? and a Coin from the one on the right. Leap the narrow Pit and go up the Staircase, then down the three steplike Ledges on the other side, using the top one as a launch pad to stomp a Lakitu if necessary. Stop on the bottom one and position yourself under the rightmost Block of the middle Ledge. (If you're Super Mario, you'll have to press the controller down to get the hero to squat, then inch him under.) Hit up repeatedly for multiple Coins. When you're finished here, go right, jump the Pit, rush up the Staircase, leap to the ultra-high Wall beyond, and hurl yourself toward the top of the Flagpole.

6/2: There's nothing to find, and no one will attack until after you pass the first Pipe. There's a Troopa to the right: fireball or stomp it, then go down between the two Pipes and jump up. You'll reveal an Invisible Block with a Coin. Get on top of that Block, jump again, and you'll find a multiple Coin Block. While you're doing all of this, be careful not to scroll the left Pipe off the screen: once you've collected these goodies, you're going back. Enter the Pipe on the left and drop into a Coin room. Once you've cleaned it out, exit; hop to the next Pipe, battle the Paratroopas, go to the next Pipe, fight the Buzzy beyond, and stand under the rightmost Block of the Ledge overhead. Hit it for a power-up, then jump onto the Ledge and up to the Pipe on the right. You can go into the Pipe and visit an underwater world, or you can wait and access a Sky Bo-

nus; the latter is recommended. If you take the
seafaring route, you'll be fighting only Bloopers until after you've passed the two Elevator/Whirlpool
Pits and the two smaller Pits beyond. Then the
Cheep-Cheeps join the fray.

If you remained on the surface world, there are
Goombas on the other side of the Pipe, and absolutely *nothing* of value for a while. You'll pass under a Pipe built on a Ledge in the air, jump two
small Pipes, leap a slightly larger one . . . and then
the good stuff starts. Stand between the Pipe you
just jumped and the one to your right, leap up, and
an Invisible Block will materialize with a Coin.
Climb onto the Block, and butt the rightmost Block
of the Ledge overhead. A Beanstalk will appear;
climb it and clean out the Coins in the Sky Bonus.

You're a thrill-seeker and didn't go cloud-
hopping? Here's what you'll find on the ground.
Jump from the Invisible Block onto the tall Pipe to
the right, kill the Buzzy below, and pass over three
Pipes until you reach the Pipe built on a Ledge
above you. Follow these directions carefully or
you'll be Buzzy-breakfast, since there's an infesta-
tion of the creatures to the right of the next Pipe—
this, by the way, is the Pipe from which you'll
emerge if you took the underwater route. Jump onto
that Pipe and leap up to the left, onto the right side
of the Ledge on which the "floating" Pipe is built.
Vault from there to the lone Block high overhead,
then hop from there to the Ledge beside it. From
here, it's an easy drop to safe ground on the other
side of Buzzyland.

There's zilch to be found in the next two Pipes, but you'll want to get on the second, jump to the Ledge on the right, and position Mario on the right side so that his foot is standing on air. Do a diagonal jump up against the left side of the Ledge overhead, and you'll get yourself a Starman. Jump to the Ledge on the right, drop down to the Staircase, and leap to the Pipe on the other side of the Pit. This Pipe leads to a Coin room, complete with a power-up Block over the Exit Pipe. When you leave, you'll be much farther along . . . though we can't go there yet: if you took the Sky Bonus trail, it'll be letting you off right about here. Hence, beyond the Pipe is a Wall with Goombas on the ground to the right; the Ledges overhead are useless—except as platforms from which to attack Goombas. Once you polish off these creeps, you'll encounter a small Buzzy army under the Pipe built on a Ledge. That Pipe has nothing to offer, nor does the large one to the right. The next Pipe over is the one from which you'll emerge if you went into the Coin room. A trio of Pipes follows, after which Paratroopas guard the round's final Staircase. It's your call whether you want to zap them from the Pipe or the ground.

6/3: For the first half of your trek, you won't face a single living foe. But that doesn't mean you can take things easy—not by a long shot! After hopping across the first three Mushrooms, using the vertically-moving Elevator to collect Coins at the top of the screen—you'll have to hop up from the Elevator to snare 'em—and hopping onto the fourth

Mushroom, you'll need to make a *very* precise jump from that Mushroom to a Springboard below to a horizontally-shifting Elevator above. Collect the Coins and hop to the next three Elevators, all moving horizontally . . . but at different speeds, just to make your life miserable. If you have trouble getting from the first Elevator to the second, you can drop to the Mushroom below, jump to the Mushroom on the right, and try to leap *left* onto the second Elevator. Naturally, it's easier making the jump from Elevator one to Elevator two without missing! The ? above the fourth Elevator contains a power-up: time your bopping of the Block so that you can catch the item as you leap from the fourth Elevator to the next lift, which moves vertically. You can rest for a moment on the Mushroom to the right of the vertical Elevator, then it's on to a duo of Balancing Elevators. To get the floating Coins between the two platforms of the first Elevator, go at once to the right edge of the left platform and hop to the right when the two sides are level, collecting the money as you leap.

When you get off the second pair of Balancing Elevators, try to do so when the right platform is high enough so you can get the floating Coins from the tall Mushroom. Leap to the Mushroom on the right, watching out for the debut of this level's Bullet Bills. However, you can actually *use* the projectiles if you've got nerves of steel—or a brain of soft clay. Hop two Mushrooms over and you'll see some floating Coins. You *can* try going to the tall Mushroom two Mushrooms over and leaping to the left

. . . *or* you can wait until a Bill passes, leap up, and use it as a stepping-stone to fling yourself up at the Coins. It's a dangerous maneuver, but by now, hopefully, you'll have a few Marios to sacrifice in the name of adventure! Continuing from that tall Mushroom, there's a Springboard on the Mushroom below, to the right. Use it to get to the horizontally-moving Elevator above. (Don't jump from the Mushroom right to the Springboard: drop to the Mushroom on which the Springboard is resting and *then* hop on. You'll have much more control over how high and how far to the right you bounce. If you're smart, you'll go from that lift to the thin Mushroom below; if you're reckless, you'll try to jump right from the Elevator to the Balance Elevator beyond. Get the Coins between them as before, and try real hard to hop onto the tall Mushroom beyond. If you land on the small one, you're going to find it difficult getting to the Mushroom on the right. Once on that latter Mushroom, take a deep breath and hop quickly across the four Elevators to the right. These platforms don't move . . . until you step on them. (That Bowser's a real joker!) Then they plummet like a lead Mario. Obviously, you should try to sweep up the Coins by the second and fourth lifts . . . but not at the expense of a Mario! The fourth collapsing Elevator leads to a tall Mushroom from which the top of the Flagpole is easily accessible.

6/4: Aaargh! More Fire Arms await! You should be pretty good at slipping through these by now . . .

though leave it to Bowser to add a new twist to the
challenge! The Podoboos on this level come more
frequently than before, while the ceiling in the Fire
Arm corridor is lower than you're used to! At least
the flames on the bottom of the corridor all turn
the same way (counterclockwise). Only the eighth
and tenth of the eleven Fire Arms, situated in the
ceiling, move clockwise. Begin by leaping the first
Pit and slipping past the Fire Arm when it hits the
three o'clock position. When the second Fire Arm
is at the nine o'clock position, jump the next Pit—
Podoboos first appear here—bop the ? for a power-
up (getting on top of the Block if you need to escape
the return of the Fire Arm), then hop the next Podoboo Pit. Just make certain that while you're
watching the Fire Arm below, you don't accidentally leap into the Fire Arm turning on the other
side of the third Pit. Use a stop-and-go technique to
get through the corridor; as soon as you clear the
last Fire Arm, watch for the flaming breath of the
not-quite-Bowser. Duck into the Pit and uncover
the six Invisible Blocks and Coins using the same
pattern from the Pit in 1/4. Now all you have to do
is beat Bowser to continue . . . a tougher task than
ever, since the shellhead is not only surrounded by
Podoboos, but is tossing Hammers. (Just to give you
something *not* to look forward to, all the remaining
Bowsers have that nasty habit!) You're going to
have to do some fancy footwork not only to get to
the Elevator above Bowser, but to *survive* up there,
since the Hammers' arcs carry them to the lift. Be

brave and alert, get the Axe, and drop the annoying creature into the Podoboo Pit!

7/1: If you've had trouble with Bullet Bills before—well, as Jolson once crooned, "You ain't heard *nothin'* yet!" In fact, if you don't get along with these creatures, you'd do well to go back to 4/2 and warp ahead to World Eight! This realm's a nightmare! Not only are there ten—yes, *ten!*—Turtle Cannons in this realm, but the second, fifth, and tenth are double-decker Turtle Cannons, firing two parallel Bills at a time. The trick to surviving this level is to get on top of one Cannon, jump over the Bullet Bill coming from the next *or* leap down and press down on the controller to duck, run toward the next Cannon, get on top of it, etc. Oh—and while you're busy doing all of this, you've also got to bop, blast, or evade Paratroopas, which begin falling at once.

The first part of the level—with the Bills and Paratroopas—is pretty straightforward. Atop the first double-decker Turtle Cannon is a Ledge, with a power-up inside the leftmost Block. You'll have to be on top of the Cannon to get it. Following the third Cannon you'll find four ?'s, all of them Coins; the problem here is that the Paratroopas will corner you under the Ledge . . . and, if you kill one and toss its Shell, there's no room for you to jump up when it comes ricocheting back. (Even if you do jump, there are the Bills on *both* sides to worry about.) Four Coins just doesn't seem worth the effort, but if you're determined to go for them, take

the two on the left and get out, cross over the Ledge
on top, then drop down and get the two on the right.
If you try to get all four in one trip, *somebody's*
going to cream you! When you come to the Cannon
located on an overhead Ledge, bop the Block to the
right of the central Block for multiple Coins ...
between Bills coming at you from the left and right!

Things get a *bit* less relentless after you leap the
Pit. The Hammer Brothers await on the other side
of the first Pipe. If you can't fireball them, you can
avoid them by *immediately* racing underneath
them, or you can wait until they come down from
the Ledges and jump on to one to run past them.
(There's nothing in the two Ledges overhead, so
don't waste time looking!) Get onto the next Pipe,
leap up to uncover an Invisible Block with a 1-Up,
then drop to the right side of the Pipe to catch it—
taking care not to scroll the Pipe off to the left, or
get plugged by the Bills coming from the right. Enter the Pipe and collect the Coins; when you exit,
you'll have left the Cannon and some Troopas behind. You're not quite home-free yet (you didn't
think you were, did you?): there's a Cannon to the
right. Actually, it's pretty easy to get on top of this
one and to leap, from there, to the Pipe beyond.
Deal with the Hammer Brothers here as you did
the ones before—again, there's nothing to get in the
Ledges—hop on the Wall, go from there to the top
of the Cannon, and jump onto the Ledge to the
right.

There's a power-up in the single Block overhead,
and a Springboard below to get to it. If you use it,

chances are good Bullet Bill will catch you in mid-leap. Instead, try standing on the right edge of the Ledge—one foot on thin air—and leaping up against the overhead Block after a Bill has come and gone. When you fall down after hitting the Block, skew Mario so that he comes down on the bottom of the Staircase to the right. Failing that, try to fall to the left of the Springboard; if you hit the Springboard itself, you may bounce right into an oncoming Bill! If you landed to the left of the trampoline, hop over it and the Pit to the Staircase. At the top of the Staircase, wait until the Buzzys on the next Staircase have gone to the ground, then leap across. Climb, hit the Flagpole, and move on!

7/2: Compared to the world you just left, this one is like a day at the beach . . . literally. It's another underwater world, and there are no real surprises. The layout and menaces are the same as 2/2; if you got through that, you should have no trouble here.

7/3: The layout here is identical to 2/3, although there are more menaces. The Troopas first attack when you reach the second Bridge; you'll be beset by Cheep-Cheeps and Paratroopas on the third. It's recommended that you use the Troopa Shells to bash the foes up ahead. After the third Bridge and until you pass the Mushroom, you'll only have Troopas to deal with. The sixth Bridge has a ? above it, with a power-up inside. You won't be able to reach the Mushroom from here unless you go to the left a bit and take a running leap; make sure you

get the floating Coins while you're in transit. After
the first tiny Bridge, you'll face two Bridges
guarded by Paratroopas. They don't go low enough
to bother Mario, but Super Mario will have to kill
them or do a lot of crouching to get by! Watch out
for the underhanded, and underfoot, Cheep-Cheeps
when you cross the three small Bridges near the
end; they can butt you to your doom. Once you reach
the downward-leading Staircase before the last pit,
no other foes will attack.

7/4: This is a round of dead-ends, and if you make
a wrong move—bye-bye Mario. But you *won't* make
a wrong move if you follow these directions carefully. Do so, and the level will be a breeze. After
walking down the Staircase, you'll come to two sta-
tionary Elevators which fall when you step on them.
Obviously, get on and off fast, taking care to avoid
the Podoboos spitting up from the Pit below. When
you reach the Wall on the other side, go down and
follow the corridor until you reach a thin Ledge
overhead. Jump up onto it—*not* onto the one above—
and, when you come to the end, hop up to the Wall
ahead. Travel along it until it ends, then drop to
the small Wall below. Hop up to the small Ledge
on the right, timing your jump so that the Fire Arm
doesn't charbroil you. Quickly leap to the Ledge
above the Fire Arm—it can reach you here, so don't
dawdle!—and then to the long Ledge beyond. Hop
the Pit to the small Ledge on the right, go *down* to
the Ledge below, go left, drop to the floor, and come
right passing under the Ledge. Hop up to the *lower*

Ledge on the right. At the end of this Ledge, jump
to the Ledge on the upper right, then drop to the
Ledge below. Go left, drop off the side, come back
under the Ledge, and leap up to the next Ledge on
the right. Continue straight to the end of this long
Ledge, then jump down. There's nowhere to get
trapped now, so just move ahead, watching out for
Bowser's fire. Again, Bowser's hurling Hammers
now, so you'll have to deal with those . . . and, unfortunately, there's no Elevator to help you get past
him. You're best bet is to run under him when he
jumps, taking care not to get singed by the Podoboos below.

8/1: Here it is: the final world! The rules change
here a bit. For one thing, if Mario dies, the next
Mario isn't just set back a bit: he returns to the
start of the region. Furthermore, you have much
more territory to cross, but no more time in which
to do it. In other words, you're going to have to
hustle! And you're going to have to do it with far
fewer power-ups available to you than ever before.
   Goombas and Buzzys are the first to attack, and
they do so immediately. After you pass the first
Pipe, you'll have to deal with Troopas and cross five
narrow Pits—hold down the B button to run over
them without falling—with Goombas and Troopas
waiting on the other side. Leap the tall Pipe and,
if you haven't been hurt, jump up between the Pipes
to get a 1-Up. Leap the Pipe to the right and the
one beyond that, then drop down the next Pipe to
enter a Coin room. Make sure you jump up one

Block left of the Exit Pipe to collect multiple Coins.
When you leave—having avoided a herd of Goombas by going underground—you'll have to cross a
field of Troopas. Leap onto the next Pipe for a re-
spite, battle the Goombas beyond, then hop onto
the Wall to the right. There's a long Ledge ahead:
slip under it, dispatching the Paratroopas below,
then leap up beneath the Ledge, below the second
Block from the right. You'll uncover an Invisible
Block with a Coin. Jump on that and leap straight
up again to collect multiple Coins.

Leave via the Wall on the right and cross the five
narrow Pits here, dueling Paratroopas as you go.
When you reach the next Ledge, leap up to claim
the Starman in the third Block from the left. Race
over the next three Pits, bash the Troopas beyond,
and get atop the small Wall. Slip down to the other
side and get a healthy running start so you can
clear the wide Pit ahead, grabbing the floating
Coins as you cross. Goombas await you on the other
side, so start fireballing as you leap. Carefully hop
from Pipe to Pipe—there are three—then battle the
Goombas and Buzzys between the last Pipe and the
Staircase. It's a pretty long stretch, so be on your
toes! More Buzzys await on the other side of the
Staircase, along with two Pits: be alert when you
jump the first, putting on the brakes—that is, pressing left on the controller—lest you slide off the right
side of the extremely narrow plateau between them.

There are two Walls on the next plateau, with
Troopas marching between them; they shouldn't be
much of a challenge. On the other hand, the super-

narrow plateau between the next two Pits *does* post
a problem. Run and leap hard *and* high so that you
can use the controller to make minor course correc-
tions as you descend. (If you can get the floating
Coins over each Pit, great! But they certainly aren't
worth risking Mario's life for.) Hopping from that
narrow plateau isn't too difficult—certainly not as
tough as it was getting *on* the plateau—and you'll
make quick work of the Troopas on the other side.
There are no foes after the first Pipe; when you pass
the second, you've got some fancy jumping to do.
There are four thin Walls, each higher than the
last and with a bottomless Pit between them. There
are no shortcuts: you need to do some Gold Medal–
caliber jumping here, or you'll perish! When you
reach the last Wall, take a long, hard jump and
you'll hit the top of the Flagpole.

8/2: This level is the Pits . . . literally. And you also
have Lakitus and other creatures to deal with, so
gird yourself for a struggle! Paratroopas rain down
from the word go and, when you leap the first narrow Pit, the first Lakitu shows its goggle-eyed
kisser. Hence, get to the top of the Staircase as
quickly as possible in order to crown the Lakitu
and avoid the Paratroopas. But don't rest on your
laurels: a Lakitu will dog you on the other side. Use
the row of ?'s as a place to fight it, if need be. (There
are Coins in all the ?'s; don't bother with them if
you don't need them.) Cross the Pit and hit the
Springboard so you can bash the Ledge overhead:
the second Block from the left contains a 1-Up. As

you cross the next five Pits, there will be nothing
but those Pits and Paratroopas to bother you. When
you approach the sixth Pit—the one with the small
Ledge overhead—a Turtle Cannon will loom to your
right. The best thing to do is get on that narrow
Ledge and take a big leap to the top of the Cannon,
jumping any Bills that come from the next Cannon
to the right—and also blasting the Paratroopas that
will be falling. Get off the Cannon between Bills,
run past the second Cannon, leap and hit the right
side of the next Ledge for a power-up, then get on
top of the third Cannon. Clear out the Buzzys ahead
for points, get on the Ledge to the right—jumping
over incoming Bills from the right—and, in quick
succession, jump on top of the Cannon that is low
to the ground, destroy the Buzzys ahead, stop as
long as you can under the Ledge with the Cannon
on it, hopping up and down—the middle Block has
multiple Coins—then take a big leap onto the Cannon in front of you. Duck any Bills from behind as
you deep-six Paratroopas falling to the right, then
go over the Pipe that lies ahead. Hop the narrow
Pit (easy!), get up on the Pipe, and—if this is your
first time here—hit the Pause button and study
what lies ahead.

There are two narrow Pits and one vast one; com-
pose your spirit and wipe your palms before you try
to get across. When you begin your crossing, don't
bother going to the first narrow plateau, but go
right to the second; it's one less jump you'll have to
take. After that, there's no way around it: you'll
need a hefty leap to get to the next landing. For-

tunately, it doesn't have to be pretty or precise—just *long*. Once you're over, go into the first Pipe and collect the Coins in the treasure room. Use the same rather complicated pattern you used in 5/1, since this room is the same. Do so quickly, though: remember, time is short in the eighth world. Sadly, the Exit Pipe lets you out just a short hop from where you entered. Immediately ahead are Paratroopas and a Cannon; position yourself on the right edge of the Pipe, use the B button to accelerate, and take a huge leap at least onto the top of the Cannon—or, even better, over the Cannon and the Pit beyond it. The jump *can* be made. Just watch out for the Goombas—and the Bills coming from behind—when you land. Obviously, you should try to land *on* the Goombas rather than beside them. Climb the Staircase quickly—there's another Cannon ahead—and avoid the Buzzys below by jumping onto the top of the Cannon. Leap over the Paratroopas to the Staircase beyond, then carefully jump from the top step to the pair of Walls and the Flagpole.

8/3: We haven't talked much about the B (acceleration) button and using it in conjunction with the A (jumping) button to make truly miraculous leaps. But you'll need 'em both now more than ever before. With Paratroopas and Bullet Bills greeting you the instant you set foot in this realm, waste no time taking a Herculean jump to the towering Wall in front of you. Without slowing down, leap the Pit ahead—there's a Cannon in its depths—to the next

Wall. Stop at the right edge. There's a Pipe below, two Ledges to the right of it, and the ever-rotten Hammer Brothers marching to and fro. Your goal is the Staircase beyond—one whose *back* is facing you (the stairs lead away from you, down to the right). The fastest way to get to the Staircase is to cross the top Ledge and drop down. If you travel along the ground, you'll have to make an awkward leap up and around the overhead Ledge on your way to the top step. (You'll also be able to get a power-up from the bottom Ledge, second Block from the right ... but it's a death-defying route!) Wait until the Hammers of the infamous duo aren't reaching the top Ledge, or watch for a break in the flurry—then B and A button your way to the Ledge and rocket across to the Staircase.

Jump from the Staircase to the next fat Wall ahead, and then to the two Walls beyond. Paratroopas will be falling all over the first two Walls, but you should be able to handle them. When you leap, try scudding across their backs to drop them. Continue running till you reach the third Wall, after which there's a thin, lower Wall beyond which are two Ledges *and* the Hammer Brothers—virtually the same setup you just suffered through. If you want the power-up in the upper Ledge, get down onto the lower Wall and hop to the top of the lower Ledge when you can. The power-up is in the second Block from the left. However, a wiser battle plan is to take a power leap from the Wall you're on to the upper Ledge and, from there, over the Pipe and two Pits beyond to the next big Wall. When you alight, the welcoming committee will consist of Troopas and Hammer Brothers. Keep the fireballs flying and be prepared to leap when necessary, and scoot ahead when you can. Cross the Pit to the next big Wall, where there are "only" Hammer Brothers to maul you. There's an Invisible Block a step in from the right side; hit it for multiple Coins. The final Staircase is a pip: three floating Blocks and a small Ledge, with the Flagpole beyond. If you can build up a good head of steam, leap right from the Wall to the top Ledge. Otherwise, you'll have to drop to the ground and take the steps one at a time. Tricky going, that!

8/4: This is it! The final level, the showdown with the real Bowser, and (fingers crossed!) the rescue of Princess Toadstool! In terms of layout, the level couldn't be simpler: just Pits and Pipes. But there are no power-ups, and a slew of foes—but happily, not the Hammer Brothers—so put your senses on maximum alert as you proceed!

The first "delight" is a Pit spitting Podoboos. You can't fail to notice it: the flames come up at you when you start down the first Staircase. A power jump from the top step to the other side of the Pit is recommended. Since time is short, leap the Pipe and *run* here; there are no foes until after you jump the second Pipe. Blast or leap the Goombas there, then ride the horizontally-shifting Elevator across the Pit. Enter the next Pipe and you'll zoom ahead a considerable distance; when you emerge, get onto the next Pipe, kill the Buzzys to the right, leap to the Pipe on the right, cut down the Paratroopas as you jump onto the Pipe beyond, then take a moment to assess the situation. You've got a Pit at your feet, Paratroopas beyond, and a mission to accomplish. See the floating Pipe ahead? When the coast is clear, position yourself midway between the Pit and the Pipe, jump up, and uncover an Invisible Block. You'll get a Coin, but more important, you'll be able to use that Block to get up to the Pipe. Doing so, you'll cut a substantial distance from your journey *and* avoid a flurry of Paratroopas.

When you leave the Exit Pipe, step up onto the Wall and watch out for the Cheep-Cheeps which begin attacking at the next Pipe to the right. As soon as you clear the next Pit, you'll find a Pipe that leads to an underwater world. There is *no* benefit to going down here, other than to slay Bloopers for points. You won't find any power-ups, you don't cut any mileage off your trek, and you'll have five nasty Fire Arms to deal with—no Whirlpools, though. All in all, you'd be wiser to stay aboveground. If you stayed out of the Pipe, you'll pass four more Pipes, and then the Hammer Brothers will attack. If you took a swim, they'll appear one Pipe after you exit. In either case, these Hammers are the elite guards of King Bowser, who lurks not too far in the distance. There's no way around the Hammers except to go *through* them. If you lack fireball power, it'll be awfully tough to stomp on them ... but you'll have no choice. Making the top of the Pipe your staging area is the best tack, since it enables you to back off to the left if need be, to get additional height when leaping the Hammers, and also to jump on the Brothers' heads the *instant* they stop throwing their weapons. Finishing them off, you'll have to leap a Pit with Podoboos, after which it's Bowser time! There's no new advice to offer regarding the master monster; as in previous worlds, you'll have to get under or over him—under is easier—although his attack is somewhat more relentless now. When you accomplish this, you'll be rewarded with the real Princess Toadstool . . . and the thanks of a grateful kingdom!

Parting Notes:

In closing, here are some helpful hints and an interesting sidebar.

Ever lose your last Mario and wish you could continue in the same world? All you have to do is push down the A button and *hold* it down as you press Start. This won't keep you in the same *realm* . . . just the same *world*. Still, it beats going back to the beginning. However—

If you want to stay alive and thus avoid having to continue, you can do so by having a slew of Marios in reserve. Back in 3/1 there's a Staircase with Troopas at the very end of the realm. If you jump onto the *left* side of the last Turtle's Shell, that will freeze it beneath you. Each time you leap up on the pinned tortoise, you'll be rewarded with a 1-Up. Just make sure you don't acquire more than 100 Marios in reserve, ever, or the computer will automatically slaughter them *all*! (Must've been programmed by Bowser.)

Finally, you've noticed the fireworks that go off whenever you enter the castle at the end of each area? But did you know that the number of fireworks you get depends upon the last digit of your time remaining? If you end the round with a 1, 3, or 6, that's how many bursts go off. What's more, you get 500 points for every blast! If you get any other number—sorry, no fireworks.

SUPER MARIO BROS. 2

Objective:

Bowser may be gone, but the universe will never want for tyrants. This time the fiend is Wart, who's subjecting the world of Subcon to the monsters created by his Dream Machine. Heroic Mario and Luigi volunteer to stop the wicked one, and this time they're not alone: they're joined by the brave Princess Toadstool and Toad.

Gameplay:

As they venture through the seven worlds of Subcon—twenty levels in all—players can be any one of the four characters, which offer the following abilities: Mario is an okay jumper who weakens slightly when he's carrying something; Luigi is a better jumper, but weakens more than Mario when he's lugging something; Toad is a so-so jumper, but doesn't lose any of that ability when he's toting something; and Princess Toadstool can levitate for nearly a second. The game is for one player only, although you can switch characters between levels.

There are many more weapons at your disposal than there were in *Super Mario Bros.* The most important of these are:

- Mushroom Blocks: can be used to build Staircases or to bop enemies.
- Mushrooms: power you up as in other Mario games.
- Vegetables and Unripened Vegetables: use 'em to bop your foes. Collect five vegetables and you'll earn a Stopwatch, which will briefly freeze your adversaries.
- Bombs: use them to blast creatures or Walls, but if you throw them too soon, they may not work the way you wanted, and if you hold them too long *you* may not work at all!
- POW: destroys all enemies around you.
- Rockets: ride them over your enemies.
- Turtle Shells: it isn't bowling for dollars, it's bowling for survival as you find these under Grasses and use them to knock down beasties.
- Cherries: just hanging around in the air, these can be plucked; get at least five of them, and you'll bring on—
- Starman: as in the previous game, he makes you invincible.
- Potion: opens the door to Subspace, where you can reap all sorts of riches.

- 1-Ups.
- Coins.

One additional power that Mario has in this game is the ability to stomp most of his foes, then pick them up and toss them at other creatures who want to trim his mustache. This power will be discussed below, where appropriate.

Points:
There are no points and no timer. (Phew! Who needed the pressure?)

Strategies:
World by world and level by level, like Henry V, we go once more unto the breach! (Note: use Mario for all of the worlds, except for the following: Luigi for 2/1, 4/1, and 5/3, and Princess Toadstool for 3/1 and 4/2. To be candid, poor Toad isn't really a help on any level . . . though you might want to give the frog a try whenever you know you've got to carry Potion a long distance, such as in 1/3.)

1/1: You're falling, but that's okay: there's a multitiered Hill below you. What's *not* so okay is that there are Shyguys on several levels. Fortunately, their population is pretty thin and you won't have any trouble getting to the Vegetable growing on the right side of the third plateau down. Finish up quickly here and head to the door at the bottom right of the screen. In the next room you'll find these objects in the following order: a Vegetable, an Unripened Vegetable, and a Vegetable. The Shyguys here are easily crunched. On the right side of the big Hill, climb the Vine and claim the three Unripened Vegetables from the left, then pull the Potion from the ground on the right. It will allow you to access Subspace, where, among the Coins, you'll also get yourself a Mushroom. The thing about Potion, however, is that you should try and use it where you see the most Grasses; like Vegetables and other items, Coins and Mushrooms are hidden beneath sprigs in Subspace. Since your time in this night-like dimension is limited, why use the Potion somewhere else and waste seconds racing to the Grasses?

Except for the hanging Cherries and an occasional Shyguy, there's nothing much happening until you reach the next Hill. All of the Grasses here and on the Log Bridge beyond give forth Unripened Vegetables. After crossing the Log Bridge, you'll come to a Waterfall with three Logs bobbing roughly side by side. Jump on these as you did the Elevators in the first Mario game. There are Unripened Vegetables in the Grasses on the other side, a Bomb at the foot of the Hill, and a Turtle Shell in the ground to the right of it. After the next small Hill you'll find a Vegetable and then an Unripened Vegetable. You'll find the same two items in the Hill just ahead ... hardly worth the effort to get them. After crossing the next Log Bridge, you'll come to a door. Enter it. If you don't, you'll miss out on an exciting region—and a shortcut to a more distant section of 1/1! When you enter the room via the bottom door, pull the two Vegetables from the ground, then continue *left*. Hop on the Wall and climb the Vine. You can also enter this room through the door on the second level of the Hill, to the right. There are no Grasses *inside*, but to the right of the room you'll find, from the left, Potion and two Vegetables. You'll have a Shyguy or two to battle up here, but the Potion will give you additional wealth—so it's your call. Whichever entrance you take, your next move will be to jump hard to the left to cross the Waterfall. Climb the Walls—disposing of the Shyguy there—and pull up either of the Grasses for a Bomb. Hurl it down the ladder, blowing up the Wall on the left. (Note: if you mess up during the procedure, leave the Hill chamber and reenter; everything will be as it was before you went in.) Go through the door in the chamber below and you'll be spirited to the end of the level. Just climb the *big* Wall to the left and you'll be ready for a showdown with the boss of this level, Birdo.

If you *didn't* enter the room in the Hill, you should still go to the upper level, pulling out the above-mentioned Grasses to the right of the door and continuing *right*. All the Grasses ahead of you are Unripened Vegetables, after which you'll come to a Vine. Climb it and get off on the Shyguy-infested, multitiered Hill. As you ascend, there are four Grasses to pluck here. From the bottom, they're an Unripened Vegetable, a Vegetable, and another two Unripened Vegetables. When you reach the top of the Hill, hop up to reach the lowest Vine, then climb, shifting to neighboring Vines when Clouds get in the way. Keep an eye out for the Vine-clinging creature, the Hoopster; it'll prevent your ascent if above you, but will help you up if below you. Switch Vines in order to use the little dream-thing to your advantage.

You'll know you've reached the top of the tallest Vine: it stops, and there are Clouds to the left and right. Go right, and you'll reach Birdo's Mountain. Unlike the other route, which would have taken you above and behind the boss, this one brings you face to beaked face. The feathered fiend is going to be tossing Eggs at you, but don't worry: leap up, catch them by landing on them, and throw them back. Three hits and the goose is cooked!

1/2: A new mode of transportation is introduced in this level: Pidgit's Flying Carpet. As you begin the round, it'll come bobbing along: jump on, and Pidgit will vacate the premises. (Miss the Carpet, and you won't be able to leave the starting gate!) The Carpet will be yours for ten seconds, during which time you'll duck some Beezos (winged Shyguys) while riding over a total of five Hills to the low plateau beyond. When you get off, enter the left Jar for a 1-Up, then go to the left and pluck the Grass there. It will give you Potion. (All the other Grasses on this Ledge conceal Unripened Vegetables.) Throw the Potion between the Jars and enter Subspace; you'll get a Mushroom between the Jars. When you exit the twilight realm, enter the Jar on the right and get the Key. Phanto will pursue you; get rid of the Jar denizen by putting down the Key for a moment, and the creature will go away. Head for the Hill to the right, watching out for Snifits, and use the Key to open the door.

Inside, the first five Grasses contain, from the left, a Bomb, two Vegetables, and two Bombs. More importantly, there are enough Cherries here to bring on a Starman . . . assuming you grabbed at least two prior to this. Leap the two Pits, using your invincible body to plow through Snifits and Ninjis. Upon reaching the Ladder, climb, and *don't* pull the Grass to the right for Potion . . . not yet. There are Bombs in the Grass to the left of the Ladder and to the right of the Potion Grass. Use these to blast the far right side of the Ledge, go back and get the Potion, and drop down. Use the Potion here for a trip to Subspace and the acquisition of a Mushroom. Exit the Hill chamber at the far right. Go *left* when you leave, pull out the one clump of Grass on the top of the Hill, and carry it to the *right*. Drop off the top of the Hill—still holding the Potion—to the lower Ledge, and use the Potion where you see all the Grasses. The Subspace will be *most* rewarding! Continue to the right, drop off the Hill, hop onto the big step you encounter, then enter the door. Birdo is on the other side, standing on a platform dead ahead. Well, not *quite* dead: you have to catch and toss back three Eggs. *Then* the wicked boss will be fricasseed.

1/3: If you have trouble leaping from one small Ledge to another, this level's going to be a nightmare for you! To begin, you're going to have to jump three Pits between Hills. You'll want to stay on the top levels to get the Cherries above each peak, though when you have to jump to the third Ledge, do so when the nasties on top are on the right. Grab the Cherries, then quickly drop down to the lower Ledge to avoid them. You'll have to leap up from there to cross the next Pit, which brings you to the Hill with the Log Bridge. The first Grass is an Unripened Vegetable, but the next is Potion; use it on the right side of the Bridge to get a Mushroom. Hop to the next four, small Log Bridges and you'll reach a Waterfall with three *very* narrow Logs bobbing up and down. Cross them to the next Hill. (One saving grace: if you fall from the Logs, there are narrow Hills below . . . last-ditch places to land *if* you can get to them.) There are Vegetables in the Grasses atop the next Hill, but those aren't as important as what lies beyond. Cross the two small Logs on the next Waterfall, and walk to the next Log Bridge. The first Grasses beneath it give you Potion—the second and third are Unripened Vegetables; the Grasses on the Log are an Unripened Vegetable and Vegetables. Take the Potion *back* to the Hill on the other side of the last Waterfall, and use it on the top to obtain Coins *and* a Mushroom. Or—even better—you can carry the Potion to the Jar ahead of you, to the right, and throw the vial there. Subspace will open up; if you enter the Jar then, you'll warp ahead to the *fourth* world! If you don't—

Return to the Log Bridge where you obtained the latest Potion, hop the small Waterfall, and enter the door in the brick building ahead. You'll find yourself in the center of a long vertical chamber. Hop to the Ledge below you, to the right, go down to the right again, then ascend using the right side of the three successive overhead Ledges. Go left onto the Vine and climb, make your way to the next Vine (on the right), cross to the Vine on the left, go to the next two Ledges on the left, then go up to the Ledge on the right. Get the Key from the room at the top, then climb back down, past the point where you entered the chamber, to the door in the lower right. This will take you into a horizontal chamber populated by sundry enemies and, to start, Spikes right below the Ledge on which you're standing. You'll have no problem with these, assuming you can jump to the Ledge beyond! You'll hop across a total of five not terribly wide Ledges to three sets of Bridges, stacked vertically. You'll want to get on the middle group in order to get the POW just right of center. Six Ledges follow this section—though you can skip the sixth and drop down to the Ledge below it to avoid the Spark. (Just watch out for adversaries on the right!) Go right, through the long corridor, and you'll reach a Crystal Ball; get on top of it, and you'll find yourself in the antechamber of Mouser, the boss of this world. All the Grasses in this room are Bombs; not surprising, since you must blow up the Wall on the right to get to Mouser, and then use Bombs to destroy the fiend. Three Bombs will do the trick; you can also catch the Bombs the giant rodent throws at you, and toss them back. The key is to try and get behind the monster, where you'll be close enough for the Bombs to do some damage without being endangered yourself.

2/1: You'll be slithered after by Cobrats during the desert portion of this level, so be prepared to kill or jump them. Jumping is, in fact, something you'll be doing a lot of here; the sand beneath you is quicksand, and if you tarry too long at any spot, you'll sink and die! Bypass the first Jar, which contains nothing but a Snifit and Shells. (The latter are useful as weapons, of course, but you should *not* need them here!) When you reach the oddly-shaped Wall just after the second Jar, go up and get the Potion from the first clump of Grass—the others contain Unripened Vegetables. Use the Potion, but take care not to drop the Mushroom: it'll sink in the sands if you do! After the Wall, there's nothing but Shyguys and desert until you come to the next Wall, which has a Panser shooting fireballs from the top. (Suggestion: bop the Shyguy below and toss him at the Panser.) Once you get by, cross more desert and then a magnificent golden Pyramid will loom. Enter.

The Pyramid is filled with sand, and you must dig down. Start on the right and, after a moment, you'll come to Cherries. Shift to the left and collect more Cherries a little farther down. Burrow straight down from there for a third bunch of Cherries, then dig horizontally to the right for a fourth set. You *should* have enough, now, for a Starman, which is good: Shyguys roam among the sands here, and invincibility will make your job a whole lot easier. Cut back to the left side and climb down the Ladder. Head to the door on the right, then exit the chamber and climb the Wall in the next room. Your old nemesis Birdo is waiting on the other side of the Pit: deal with the creature as before, but make sure, while you elude its Eggs, that you don't fall into one of the Pits.

2/2: You won't find anything new for a while after you pass through the door and begin the next leg of your journey: more sand, Shyguys, and Cobrats to start. Alas, the Jars hold nothing of particular importance . . . nothing *good* that is. Leap the first Jar you encounter and get on the plateau. The first clump of Grass will give you Potion—there are Vegetables in the others. Use it while you're on the plateau and collect the Coins and Mushrooms. At the end of the plateau hop from Jar to Jar, then hurry across the next plateau. As you cross this expanse, use the rib cage at the end as a Springboard if you need to keep yourself from sinking. When you reach the Rockpile, drop to the right and enter the door. You'll find yourself in a chamber with Grasses that give you a 1-Up (lower right), and Bombs (the Ledge to the left, above the 1-Up). Destroy the Wall, enter the room on the left, jump to the golden Wall, and get Potion from the Grasses second from the right on *top.* (The Grasses below, right and left, contain Vegetables; right of the Potion is a Vegetable, and left is a POW.)

When you leave the room, continue across the sands with caution: in addition to the projectile-spitting Cobrats, you'll face Pokey, a troublesome cactus. If you can't leap the green bein', grab a fallen foe—such as a Cobrat—and throw it at Pokey's head. None of the Jars in this stretch of desert is any more rewarding than the ones before. Your next challenge is a pair of Pansers sitting atop a golden Wall; either you can bring a bested enemy to throw, or you can race past them—your goal is a red Vine in the Wall beyond. Get on top of the stalk and climb *down*. It will drop you into a deep vertical chamber filled with sand, Cherries, and Shyguys. Start digging toward the right side to get the first Cherries, continue diagonally down to the right for the second batch, diagonally down to the left for the third, diagonally right for the fourth, and diagonally left for the last. Then go to the right side and head straight down to reach the door. As you make like a mole, remember: the Shyguys can only move from side to side. The door opens into a chamber where you'll climb down a set of steps to the right and—surprise!—you'll have to battle another Birdo. Although you can still use Birdo's Eggs to clobber the villain, it's recommended that you pick up the Mushrooms on the bottom level, carry them up the left to the Birdo platform above, and bombard the creature with those.

2/3: After climbing the Ladder back to the desert, head right and grab the first clump of Grass for

Potion. Carry it to the left, past the Ladder, to the small Hill, and toss the vial there. Enter Subspace to obtain Coins and a Mushroom, then go right. The next Grasses you encounter will all be Vegetables. When you come to the Hills, you'll want to enter the door atop the first Hill on the left: there's a Subspace inside, with Coins and a 1-Up. In order to get up there, however, it'll be necessary to hop on the head of a Beezo and use him as a Springboard to reach the top. To get back down to the desert, hop to the Hills on the right—the Grasses there contain Vegetables. A *really* long expanse of desert stretches before you, and Beezo attacks occur with regularity. Your destination is another huge Pyramid; enter and you'll find yourself at the top of a loooong vertical chamber. Jump to the narrow Ledge on the *left* and fall, like Alice down the rabbit hole, to the sands way below. (If you go down the right, you'll face more enemies than on this route.) The instant you hit the sand, start digging. Again, you should burrow downward diagonally to reach the Cherries: first to the right, then left, then left again, then right, then down with a slight diagonal slant to the left. When you reach the last bunch of Cherries, cut to the left and you'll hit a door. Enter and get the Key, dealing with Phanto as you did previously.

Upon obtaining the Key, dig up to the top of the sands. To the right is a door; use the Key to get in. The new chamber is a pip. It's long, and the only power-ups are Cherries. When you reach the sand,

dig down for the first Cherries, then dig straight
ahead to the right for the next one back, diagonally
down to the right for the third, and diagonally up
to the right for the fourth. Leave the sand and, at
the very end of this Pit, you'll find Cherries hanging overhead. This'll give you a Starman, enabling
you to race past the Shyguys and Panser on the
Hill ahead. There's nothing but more useless Jars,
Cobrats, and other foes in the remainder of the
chamber—nothing you haven't had to deal with before. However, when you reach the end and enter
the next room, a new challenge awaits: the mon-
strous three-headed, fireball-spitting serpent Tryclyde. Actually, dealing with the monster is easier
than it might seem. When you enter, you'll find six
Mushroom Blocks stacked to the left of the two
Ledges to the left of the creature. Form a barricade
against the fireballs by stacking three Mushroom
Blocks on the left side of the lower Ledge, and three
on the right side of the upper Ledge. Then disman-
tle the lower wall you built, carrying each Mushroom Block to the top Ledge one at a time, jumping
onto the wall you erected there, and throwing the
Mushroom Blocks at Tryclyde. Hit the beast three
times and it's a goner.

3/1: Enter the door and you'll find yourself on a
Ledge halfway down the face of a raging Waterfall.
Jump off the Ledge and literally drop to the bottom,
where you'll find a door. Enter, and the room will
offer two options, both involving Potion—tenth
clump of Grass from the left; the others are all Un-

ripened Vegetables. You can use it to collect Coins, or you can carry it to the far right side of the chamber and toss it at the Jar. Once you're in Subspace, you can enter the Jar and warp ahead to World Five. If you opt to stick around—leave the chamber by the door in the corner and you'll find yourself on the Waterfall on the side opposite the door in the Hill. Hop up and, when you reach the top of the cataract, get on Pidgit's Flying Carpet as you did before, in order to complete your ascent. Grab the Vine on top and climb to the Cloud Ledge where— if you're the Princess—you can float to the *left* to reach a secret doorway that will spirit you to the end of the level. If you're anyone else, get off the Vine on the left, have a look to the right to assess the situation—that is, where's the Shyguy?—then go right to the first Hill; your best bet for getting up there is to hop up onto the first Cloud to the right, jump up to the one on the left, move to the one on the upper right, then leap down to the Hill from there.

On the Hill are two clumps of Grass; the first contains Potion, the second an Unripened Vegetable. Use the Potion on the Hill, but be careful when getting the Mushroom: it, or you, may fall into the abyss beyond. After leaving Subspace, continue to the right, climbing the three Clouds and using the Mushroom Block on the third as a weapon, if need be. Drop onto the Hill and climb the next three Clouds. Leap ahead to the top of the two-tiered Wall—using the Unripened Vegetable on the lower tier (left) or beside the Ladder to deal with foes.

Climb down the Ladder, pull the Potion from the leftmost Grass—the others are all Unripened Vegetables—and use it here. The Mushroom will be outside the chamber; not only should you hurry to get it, you must take care: it, too, is on the edge of a cliff. When Subspace disappears, make your way to the door on the right. The Birdo you'll face here is a bit more versatile than the others: the Eggs don't move in predictable patterns, so you have to be on your toes to catch them. It's a good idea to get behind Birdo—go from the Wall to the upper Ledge and drop down on Birdo's Ledge—then bop the beast with the Mushroom Blocks you'll find there.

3/2: There's a world below your feet, but you can't get to it—not yet, anyway. Head right, picking your way through the swarms of Beezos; the only Grasses you'll find in this part of the world are two Unripened Vegetables on the far side of the first Hill. Some distance beyond that, you'll cross two POWs but *don't* use them: if you remove them and slip to the level below, you'll miss out on the Subspace on the next (and last) Hill. Hop on top: from the left, the Grasses contain Potion, a Vegetable, and a Vegetable. Use the Potion, collect the Coins and Mushroom, and beware when you emerge from Subspace: a Snifit will be waiting to attack you. Drop off the Hill to the left and use the Grasses there—both Bombs—to blast away the Blocks in the ground to the right of them. Drop through the opening, head left, and climb down the first Ladder you encounter.

Drop to the Ledge below you, hop up to the Ledge on the left, and pull the Grasses—all are Bombs—to destroy the Wall at the bottom of the Ladder. Destroy the next Wall to the left, then the two beyond that. If you need more Bombs, use the Grasses down here or climb the next Ladder to the left to the room above—a worthwhile trip, in any event: you also get a POW there. When you reach the left end of this section—you'll know you're there because you can't go any farther—jump to the Ledge on the upper right and climb the Ladder there. Go left, and descend the first and only Ladder you find. This will bring you to the other side of that Wall you'd run up against. Hop the three Pits to the left—watching out for a Shyguy attack—then climb the Ladder there. Cross the small chamber, climb down the next Ladder, and destroy the Block Wall to the left using the Bombs on the Ledge—there are three of them, and you'll probably need them all: the Wall is a sturdy one! Go through the next chamber and up the Ladder, but *don't* go all the way to the top. Just climb a few rungs, then go to the left. The Grasses, from the right, contain a pair of Vegetables, Potion, and Bomb. Use the Bomb, first, to blow up the Blocks in the floor on the right side, opening the chamber below; when you use the Potion to access Subspace, this is where the Mushroom will be. When you're finished here, climb the Ladder the rest of the way and enter the door in the middle of the room. Travel to the left for your next confrontation with the indomitable Birdo. This one's easy to kill: just hop your foe, get to the Mushroom Blocks on the left, and pelt the bird.

3/3: Upstairs you go, and through the door to a new adventure. The first Grasses you encounter—immediately after the POW—consist of Unripened Vegetables followed by a Potion on the right. Wait until you enter Subspace, get the Mushroom, and *then* get the POW: when you emerge from Subspace, you'll have *two* POWs! Except for the usual flock of foes, not much happens until you reach the door set in the side of the brick building. Enter and head left; from the right, the Grasses will give you a POW, a Shell, Potion, and another POW. Don't use the Potion here; carry it to the left. Sparks and Ninjis will attack you as you travel, but they can be stopped using the POWs. You'll pass below a door on a Ledge above—it's the first of three doors on this level, and it leads to Room Three—then pass beneath a second Ledge, and finally beneath a third Ledge. Walk past the next door and use the Potion at the Ladder. You'll be able to get a Mushroom from the Ledge above.

The second and third doors in this room lead to Rooms Two and One, respectively. (Got that? Door One leads to Three, Two leads to Two, and Door Three leads to Room One.) Entering Door One—the door on the Ledge—you'll be in a tall, vertical room in which your goal is a doorway on the upper right. Reach it by climbing staggered Ledges. The early going presents a whopper of a problem: the Jar on the fifth Ledge is producing Shyguys at an alarming rate. Since you can't beat them all, you're advised to avoid them: leap the little creeps, and shift to the left or right to get out of their way. When you reach the door, enter the small room and get the Key ... taking care not to get creamed by the Sparks or Phanto. When you're finished here, leave the way you came and head to Room One—the door on the left side of the chamber. Enter and ascend this tall vertical chamber. Your chief foes in the lower half of the room will be Sparks. Happily, you won't have to deal with them for very long: slip between them when you can, slowly but steadily making your way up the "+"-shaped Ledges to the silver Ledges to the door on the upper right. (On the way up, after the + Ledges, there'll be a flat silver Ledge, a rectangular one, then another flat one, followed by the door.) Now ... if you avoid the door and continue upward here, you will come to a long Ladder. Unfortunately, when the Ladder ends, there's no way to reach the Ladder on top of it— unless you're the Princess and can float to it. So, you have to leave the chamber via the door, enter another chamber, and come back to this room higher up, beyond the Ladders.

When you go through the door, you'll be in a new room, a long vertical chamber; this is the room you could have accessed by Door Two in the earlier three-door room. You were directed to come *this* way because it's the least dangerous route. Ascend using the silver Ledges—there will be five in all—then head to the Chain on the left and climb. When you reach the next silver Ledge, you'll notice a pair of Pansers to the right; they're bad news, because you've got to cross the platform using the Chains overhead . . . Chains sitting right in their crossfire. Just wait until there's a pause in their onslaught, then make like Tarzan and rush from Chain to Chain as fast as possible. Climb to the top of the last Chain, then cross to the left to the door. Pass through it and you'll be back in the other room, well above the Ladder section. Sparks await, but so do Cherries and Grass which contains a POW—the latter is in the silver rectangle that will shortly scroll into view in the upper left. Ascend using the silver Ledges until you reach a Ladder just left of center. Climb it to the door on top, enter, and you'll be in a horizontal level.

The first and only Grass here contains a Shell; bring it to the level's only Ledge—which you must use to cross the chasm—and use it to bowl your enemies over. When you reach the Crystal Ball at the end, you'll enter the last room of this world: the headquarters of boss Mouser and his guardian Sparks. As before, catch the Bombs and lob a half dozen of them back at the big rat to destroy him.

4/1: Much to your chagrin, you'll find a new twist here: ice! You'll be walking on it, so take care not to slip. Playing Luigi, begin your trek and keep an eye out for the Flurry or two you'll run into—or, rather, who will run into you. The first clump of Grass you'll encounter contains Potion: get it by sliding under the Ledge above it, then hopping onto that Ledge after you have the Potion. Use the magic up there, but only when Flurry isn't nearby. Get the Mushroom, and continue to the right. The Grasses there all contain Vegetables, which will be extremely useful against the Flurries. After you go down the steps and jump onto the next platform to the right, you'll find Grasses on the right. (Note: the Ledge here is not slippery.) The clump on the bottom right contains a Vegetable; the two Grasses on top contain Potion (left) and a Vegetable. Use the Potion here and get the Mushroom from Subspace. When you emerge, go to the icy Ledge on the right and drop down. The clump of Grasses here will give you a Rocket. Take it: it's your only way out of this level.

The second stage gives you more icy Ledges to negotiate. In addition to Shyguy, you'll face its new conveyance, the Autobomb, which not only homes in on you, but spits flame. Your best bet is to kill Shyguy, then hop right on top of the Autobomb, letting it give you a piggyback ride. Do this again after the Wall: get on top of the Column, hop onto Shyguy, and ride the Autobomb. There are more Flurries, more Columns, and more ice ahead . . . but nothing that will cause you to lose any sleep. At the end you'll find a Crystal Ball but no boss; a charitable gesture from the otherwise merciless Wart!

4/2: Be the Princess this level: you'll save yourself a lot of pain. To get under way, climb the Vine and go right. The word "uneventful" accurately de-

scribes this part of your journey. Oh, there are
Flurries and Beezos, and it's a good idea to get rid
of them the instant you encounter them: the Flurries will keep after you if you don't. But you should
be able to breeze through to the door at the end.
When you get there, enter and you'll find yourself
in a considerably more difficult level. Drop off the
Cloud and go *left* to the Grasses, obtaining—from
the right—two Vegetables and Potion. Now, if you
enter Subspace from the back of the Whale, you'll
find a Mushroom waiting for you. If not, you'll get
Coins. (Or, you can save your Potion and use it
ahead, at the Jar. More on this in a moment.) Either way, head right when you're finished there,
making sure you get the Cherries hanging above
the floating Ledges at the top of the screen. The
next *two* sets of Grasses both consist entirely of Unripened Vegetables, but the lone Grass on the top
of the next Wall will give you Potion. Again, enter
Subspace from a Whale if you want to get a Mushroom. Finishing up here, continue to the right. If
you kept the Potion, continue carrying it until you
reach the Jar. Use it here, enter the Jar, and you'll
warp ahead to the Sixth World. If you don't do this,
go right to the Grasses, pull them out for a Rocket
and ride to the next screen. There are Cherries behind the first Column, and the Grasses you'll encounter will give you Potion. More important is the
corridor beyond them: it's lined with Spikes, so
you'll have to board the Autobomb to get across.
Grab the Cherries as you go through and Starman
will appear, enabling you to walk right through the

Porcupo on the other side. The door at the end leads to the Birdo chamber. Since the Ledge on which the boss is standing is made of ice, you'd be wise to get on the Ledge beneath and mount your attack from there and from the low Walls on either side.

4/3: When you stroll through the door, there's a Birdo to your right and Grasses on the roof immediately overhead and on the higher roof to the right. The one on the left is Potion; Vegetables are in the other two. When you obtain the Potion, go to the Columns on the left: use the magic here and you'll find a Mushroom on top of the centermost Column. Return to the door, and instead of killing Birdo, get on top of one of the Eggs and use it as a conveyance to take you across the expanse of ocean to the right. Otherwise, you won't get across: even the Princess can't levitate *that* far! When you reach the Staircase Wall on the other side, all of the Grasses there contain Unripened Vegetables. Leap over to the thin Ledge on the right, then enter the door in the Tower. (Note: even if you're the Princess, you won't be able to vault to the next Ledge on the right. You've no choice but to use the door.) Inside is a vertical chamber; you must use the slippery Ledges to ascend, leaping and bopping Flurries as you do. Watch out for the Icicles (Spikes) on the Ledge halfway up; fortunately, they're the only ones you'll encounter in this room. The exit is located in the upper left. The door leads you to a Bridge between the two Towers; you'll find Potion (left) and a Vegetable in the Grasses on the span. Take the Potion to the *left*, climb the two Clouds to the top of the Tower, go to the Tower on the right, and use the magic there to obtain a Mushroom.

Upon entering the door on the other side of the Bridge, you'll find yourself in a Tower similar to the one you just left. Leave the Ledge on the left, then stand at the edge of the Ledge you're on. Wait until a Shyguy passes by, then jump on his head: it's the only way you'll get across the Icicles up here. Drop down the Pit beneath the Icicles—nabbing Cherries as you fall—and land on the Ledge in front of the door right at the bottom of the Pit. Inside, you'll find the Key needed to open the door at the bottom of the chamber. The Flurries in here won't present much of a challenge. In fact, once you have the Key, you can use it as a weapon! Descend along more icy Ledges to the door at the bottom, just to the left of center, and use the Key to unlock it. You'll find yourself in front of the second Tower: go right and enter the door in the third Tower. You're in a Crystal Ball room, but there's no boss—not yet, anyway. Get rid of the two Flurries, go the Mask door, enter, and you'll find a small room with the missing boss—the vile, fire-spitting Fryguy. To combat him, use the Mushroom Blocks in the room—preferably the ones on the floor. Grab one and go to the left or right corner, heave it at Fryguy, grab another and repeat. Three strikes and he'll split into four mini-Fryguys; use the Mushroom Blocks to hit and destroy these permanently—from the upper Ledges if you can, though the corners are okay too.

5/1: The first level of this world starts out easy enough . . . but then it really gets hairy! The first section offers nothing except foes—the most troublesome of which is the Panser shortly after the second Palm Tree. Getting past it between bursts, go to the end of the cliff, jump down, and hop the Pits to the *left* until you come to a door. Go in, and you'll find two Grasses right in front of you, and five clumps in the niche ahead to the right. The Grasses at your feet contain a Bomb (left) and Potion. Use the latter here for Coins. When you get to the top of the Wall, you'll notice that there's zilch ahead of you except for water and Logs. Guess how you're going to have to get across! After reaching the next Wall, you'll be faced with the most difficult challenge yet in the game: using the heads of your enemies, the Trouters, to hop across the Waterfall. You'll have to use a trio of Trouters to reach the next "oasis," another Wall. Use Logs to cross the next section of Waterfall, then Trouters, then stop when you get to the Wall with the Ledge above it. There are Grasses on that Ledge: a 1-Up on the left, Potion on the right. (Note: you'll have the easiest time getting up there if you're Luigi.) Enter Subspace and get the Mushroom from the Ledge below. Upon emerging from Subspace, continue across the Waterfall. The two-Log section at the end is the last you'll have to deal with—but make sure you deal with it *correctly*. There's a room ahead, but you don't want to go directly into it. When you're on the last Log, jump right and up: slide down the vertical passageway in order to get the Mushroom Block stuck in the center of it. You can't get this object from below. Once you hit the ground, you'll find Grasses: Potion is on the left, and the rest are Unripened Vegetables. Use the Potion here, get the Mushroom, and head right. You're in Birdo land yet again. Since the boss is now spitting fire, you have to be on your toes—and on Birdo's case! Hop the creature, get the Mushroom Block, and use it to bash the bird. You'll have to hit Birdo three times with the same Block in order to be victorious.

5/2: Travel to the right, climb the Ladder, and enter a world of darkness! The first Hill has four Grasses: a Bomb (left) and three Unripened Vegetables. When you get to the Trees beyond, you'll notice something unsettling: Hoopsters traveling up and down the trunks. You can go under 'em when they're up, or over 'em when they're down. (Over is better: you can bop them!) Shortly after the first group of Trees, you'll come to a lone clump of Grass with a Vegetable, then a higher plateau with more Trees. Beyond these Trees you'll find a Jar and more Grasses. Surprisingly, there's no Potion in the Grasses; from the left, there's just a Bomb, two Unripened Vegetables, and a Vegetable. Ah, but there *is* the Jar! Enter with a Bomb, blow a hole in the floor, and drop to a secret room below! There's a clump of Grass and (voilà!) it's Potion. Take it, leave the Jar, and use it when you're outside. At the end of the plateau jump down to lower ground and continue right; there's nothing good here, so don't dawdle. Hop the small Pit to the next narrow little Hill, and use the Bomb from the Grass there to make the Tree enemy-free. Climb and jump to the next Hill, then be prepared to jump from one Tree to another—each of which has a Hoopster on it. It's best to make this double jump when the nearest Hoopster is high on the Tree and the second Hoopster is low: you have to go from the second Tree to the rather high Hill beyond, so you want to be able to climb if need be . . . tough to do with the Hoopster coming *down* on you! There's a Pit and a *very* narrow Wall after the Hill, so jump to the latter with care. Get on the Tree beyond, and this time kill the Hoopster: you're going to need its carcass to bop the Panser on the next Hill. Get on the Panser-free Hill, jump onto the next Tree, and get to the Hill beyond. There's a small Hill rising from this larger one, and you'll find Grasses on it: two Vegetables with a Bomb sandwiched between them. All will come in handy here. After this nub of a Hill, you'll encounter two more Grasses: the one on the left has an Unripened Vegetable, and the one on the right a POW. After crossing the big Pit beyond, you'll come to a Vine. Start climbing, video-gamer!

As you ascend, a second Vine will appear to the left. Don't take it. Although a pair of Snifits and a Beezo will come at you, there's a Hoopster waiting on the left Vine: if you shift there, Hoopster will attack and you'll have nowhere to retreat. At least the Snifits (on the sides) and Beezo (comes from beneath you) can be dealt with rather easily. Get off on the Cloud at the top of the Vine and go right, into the door. There's a Bridge whose center Block is a POW: remove it and drop through. As you free-fall—quite a distance, so don't be alarmed—be prepared to shift left and right to avoid the Icicles that poke up from cliffs along the way. When you finish passing through the narrow neck of the canyon, begin shifting to the right. There's a Ledge with a door; if you miss it, you stand a good chance of landing in the Trouter-filled waters and perishing. Going through the door, you'll find yourself in (ta-ta!) Birdo's presence. In addition to the typical Egg-tossing contest, one really good tack to use here is to stay to the left of the break in the Bridge, grab Trouter when it appears, and toss *it* at Birdo.

5/3: As William Dozier used to say, "Another challenge for Luigi!" (Actually, he said it about the Green Hornet ... but new times demand a new hero!) You'll need Mario's brother's jumping skills for this world. Go right to the Ladder, climb, and you'll find yourself under a Ledge that contains a Jar. Jump up—Mario and Toad will have a tough time doing this—and use the Potion in the Grass to the right of the Jar (there are Vegetables in the two clumps to the left). You can now enter the Jar in Subspace and warp to World Seven; the choice is yours! (Halfway through this level, you may *wish* you'd warped ahead.) If you stay here, continue right. Just after the Palm Trees are three Grasses: Potion on the left, two Vegetables on the right. Use the Potion here, or bring it with you. Watching out for Albatosses above unleashing Bob-Ombs in your direction—remember: these dudes kill by touch *or* by exploding—move ahead, collecting Cherries. When you reach the Hill, you'll find Grasses on top with Potion (left) and Vegetables (all the rest). Whether you use this Potion or carried the previous Potion with you, be sure to use it at the foot of the Hill in order to obtain a Mushroom. The next landmark you'll encounter is a T-shaped Log formation, by which time you should have collected enough Cherries to bring on Starman. If you haven't—watch out! When you reach the Log Ledge in front of the Towerlike Tree, you'll be besieged by Bob-Ombs. You can plow through them if you're invincible; if not, take hip-hopping jumps to get over and past them. There's a Vegetable in the Grass patch on the Log (right side) if you need it, and another Vegetable in the clump on the Log in front of the next Tree Tower, just past the Hill. (Note: you don't want to go on those Logs if you don't have to; it's quicker to go under the first one, up onto the Hill, then under the second one—a cinch if you have Starman, but still do-able if you're just plain Luigi.)

A short plain follows the second Tree Tower, after which you'll reach a Wall with a Ledge above. Go up. There are three Grasses: two Bob-Ombs with a Potion in the center. Use the Bob-Ombs to blow up the Wall—keeping in mind that they explode much faster than ordinary Bombs, so there's no time to tarry! When you've broken the Wall, use the Potion and collect the Mushroom. Then pluck the Grass to the right of the destroyed Wall to get

a normal Bomb and blow up the Wall to the right.
This will allow you to access a Ladder—the only
way out of this region. Upon descending, you'll find
yourself in a corridor with a Jar to the right and a
Mushroom Block on top of it. When you remove the
Block, Bob-Ombs will emerge. Hurry to the left and,
when you reach the narrow Ledge at the end of the
corridor, grab one of the pursuing Bob-Ombs and
use it to destroy the Wall beneath the Ledge. (A
Shell in the lone Grass clump to the left of the Wall
will help deal with any other Bob-Ombs menacing
you.) Beyond the razed Wall you'll find Grasses;
from the left they are a Bomb, four Vegetables, and,
on the far right, Potion. Enter Subspace here to
reap the riches, then continue left. When you reach
the Pit, jump up to the Wall ahead—there's a Vegetable in the Grass clump—cross the Log in front of
the first Tree Tower (the Grass on the Log contains
a Vegetable), hop to the other Log, and enter the
door in the second Tree Tower. This new room's a
corker! It's the inside of the Tree: a vertical chamber with passages exiting left and right in the upper half. When you exit one, you reenter on the
other side of the room. That's handy, since you have
foes like a walking Panser to deal with. (If you
choose to stand and fight the Panser which attacks
shortly after you arrive, there are Mushroom Blocks
to the right, immediately above where you enter
the chamber.) The only way to get to your goal, the
top of the chamber, is to go to the bottom and then
head up the left side. In addition to the Panser,
you'll have Sparks to fight as well as a pair of Jars

that release Shyguys. There are Mushroom Blocks all over the place; throw them at the former, and use them to plug the Jars.

When you reach the top and pass through the door, you'll find yourself on a Log with Grasses to the right; there are Vegetables in all. The next two Logs contain nothing useful—which isn't the same as containing nothing at all: you have enemies here, remember! You'll need Pidgit's Carpet to cross the chasm beyond the last Log; pay no attention to the Pidgit that passes when you near the next Tree Tower. Hop onto the Log, the Grasses of which are all Vegetables. Proceed by hopping across the Clouds, then wait when you get to the first T-shaped Log edifice: there are three such structures in a row, and Birdo is on the last of them. Use the Eggs to make an omelette of the creep, then climb the Staircase beyond. Eliminating Birdo was only the first step in exiting World Five: in the next room, you've got to deal with Clawgrip. This crab digs into a pile of Rocks and throws them at you; your task is to grab them after they've landed and throw them back. Since you have to cross a narrow Pit, Rock in hand, this is one region where, conceivably, Toad would give you a *slight* advantage. However, his presence here is not worth having to suffer through the earlier stages with his meager abilities. When Clawgrip evaporates, you are ready to enter—

6/1: Well, T.E. Lawrence, here's just what you needed: more deserts, more unstable sands, and

more Cobrats. Actually, the challenge here is not
so much to survive—which is relatively easy—as to
find Key objects . . . if you get our meaning. To begin, travel to the first Jar. Kill the Cobrat, enter
the Jar, get Potion from the Grass, exit, and enter
Subspace atop the rib cage to the right of the Jar.
When the Mushroom materializes, snatch it quickly
or it'll be swallowed up by the sands. Continue to
the right, dealing with old foes, until you reach the
two Jars: use the Shell found in the first to bop the
Cobrat that emerges from the second. Frankly, this
part is pretty mundane; after the Jars, you'll cross
more desert, encountering the likes of Panser and
Pokey, as well as Grasses with a Vegetable and Potion, in that order; go right, use the Potion on top
of the golden hut at the end of the desert, and you'll
get a Mushroom. (In normal-space, the Grasses
there all contain Vegetables.) When you're done,
enter the hut and go to the edge of the Ledge. This
is the fun part: there are 21 Jars before you. If you
want to explore them all, go ahead. However, what
you need is the Key buried in the sands of the fifth
Jar from the right—you'll also find a 1-Up in the
third Jar from the left. With the Key, you'll be able
to open the door in the right side of the room. That
will lead you to Birdo's chamber: the blue bird of
unhappiness is only spitting fire and not chucking
Eggs, but that also means you can't catch them and
throw them back. What you need to do is carry the
Mushroom Blocks, one at a time, to the top of the
Staircase and toss them onto the boss. There are

only three Blocks, so don't miss, or you'll have to go down right next to Birdo to get them back.

6/2: Like 6/1, this is a short level—but fear not, 6/3 makes up for it. If you're not Luigi or the Princess, you're going to have to make a big jump to climb the second step of the Staircase in the first room. Accomplishing this and exiting, you'll be on a Ledge with one Grass (a Vegetable); the only way to get off is to ride an Albatoss. Once you're on board, soar over the Wall with the Panser and dismount when you reach the Wall with the Grasses. The Grass on the left has Potion—the right clump has a Vegetable. Enter Subspace here, then hitch a ride on a leftward-headed Albatoss—that's the only direction they'll be flying out here—and go back to the beginning. Mount an Albatoss flying to the right—only this time you won't have to get off on the Wall with the Potion. Shortly after you pass this point, a stack of Albatosses will come flying at you: it will be necessary to jump *over* the trio and land back on your Albatoss when it has flown through the flock. Leave your winged taxi when you reach the narrow Wall (the one with the Grass—a Vegetable) and hop to the Wall beyond. Pass through the door and you'll be in Birdo's chamber—we *told* you this realm was short! First, get the Mushroom Block from the ground and bring it to the Ledge directly above Birdo. Drop that one, and the one already up there, onto the big-nosed boss. Then go down, grab the handiest of those two Mushroom Blocks, and heave it at Birdo to conclude the battle.

6/3: Like we said before . . . this region's a fa
one, full of danger and nifty sights. To begin with
when you get off the Ladder, do so on the *left* side
Let yourself sink into the sands, and you'll be o
the other side of that Wall to your left. Where wil
you end up? At a door that will take you to th
Pyramid at the end of 6/3! Should you care to battl
your way through, head right off the Ladder
There's Grass with Potion at your feet, but don'
use it here: carry it to the second rib cage and ope
Subspace there. You'll find the Mushroom atop th
cactus. The only other thing you need to know abou
the desert is that there's a Bomb in the lone Gras
ahead, following the second rib cage after Sub
space; you won't need it for a Wall, so use it agains
your enemies. After entering the door in the ston
building, you'll have to play some heads-up vide
gaming. Bob-Ombs will start charging you from th
Jars, but don't panic. Grab the nearest Ladder
hang onto it, and wait until the walking explosive
detonate. (Be certain, though, that when you go u
the first Ladder, you collect the Cherries on eithe
side.) When they do, they'll take the nearest Ja
with them. Dig down at the right side of the firs
and second sandpits to get Cherries.

When you reach the sand Wall to the right—th
one standing there in defiance of the laws of grav
ity—dig to the right and then *up* to the top of th
stone Wall. Both Grasses contain Bombs. Take one
go back into the sand, use the explosive to make a
hole at the bottom of the stone Wall on the right

go back and get the second Bomb, make the hole larger, and go through. Get the Cherries on top of the sands in here; if you've gotten all the others in this room—and there's no reason you shouldn't have!—Starman will arrive. And a good thing, too: Ninji after Ninji will attack. Without invincibility, your chances of surviving are not good. Burrow up through the sands to the right, head right when you reach the stones, and pull the Grasses to get rid of the Wall in front of you. If you blew up the Wall so that a Pit was created, you can drop down— but make certain you skew Mario to the left or right, or he'll tumble to his death in the Pit below the first Pit. If you do this, however, you'll miss out on a Subspace encounter. So, instead of dropping down, go right. Skip the first Grass (the Potion) for now and get the second (a Bomb). Place the explosive at the Wall, blow it up, and ignore the next Grass (another Bomb). Take the Bomb from the Grass after that, however, and hurry down the Ladder to the right. Run to the left and use the Bomb to blow up the Wall. (All the Grasses you'll pass here are Vegetables.) If you need another Bomb, go back and get the one you skipped before—keeping in mind that it's a slightly longer distance to travel and the Bomb *may* explode before you arrive, blowing you to subatomic particles! Assuming you made it, go back now and get the Potion. Bring it down the Ladder and use it at the broken Wall; you'll have no trouble getting the Mushroom that appears. Upon emerging from Subspace, return to the Ladder. (Incidentally, while there *are* more rooms to the left, you've no reason to go to them now: there's nothing in them but Grasses containing Bombs and Vegetables.) Leave the Ladder when you've gone high enough to clear the Wall on the right, then walk to the Vine. Climb.

You're now in a realm that boasts more Vines than the Amazon! Climb up the right cliff and, when the Hoopsters are low down—they're infamously low-down, but that's another story!—hop onto the Vine on the left. When you reach the Cloud, transfer to the left again. You'll see how to proceed from here, simply by looking at the way the Vines are hanging; how you ascend also depends upon where the Hoopsters are. However, here are a few things to look out for. When you reach the first long Cloud with a series of short Vines hanging side by side, make the transfers by pushing both up and right or left on the control pad. You'll run into Shyguys and Snifits shortly after clearing the abovementioned Vines. Watch the Snifits when they shoot, and note carefully just where their projectiles go; position yourself right below that spot and, during a lull in the firing, scoot past the badsters. The last real danger spot is several Clouds up: you'll see one Vine hanging down from the left, and three from the right—they get successively shorter the farther to the right they are. Do *not* go up those Vines on the right: the Hoopsters are truly dangerous here. Stay to the left for the remainder of your ascent.

When you reach the top of the last Vine, head to the right and the golden Pyramid. (If you warped

here from the beginning of this World, you'll be to
the far right of the Pyramid, on a Cloud. To reach
the Structure, make your way to the left, across the
Clouds.) Inside the Pyramid you'll be battling
Birdo. (Gee . . . what a surprise!) And while there's
a Mushroom Block here, it's useless: you'll need to
get on top of it in order to jump to the Ledge where
Birdo is standing. So, just like in the old days, you'll
have to fight the Egg-tossing, fire-breathing monster using the captured Eggs. Upon defeating
Birdo, you'll be ushered into the presence of Tryclyde.
Truth be told, the serpent isn't as tough as it looks.
Take three Mushroom Blocks from the *right* side of
the row of Blocks and stack them one atop the other
on the Ledge in front of Tryclyde—erecting them in
the center of the Ledge is fine. When you stand on
top of these, you'll be taller than the dragon and
its flames won't touch you. Go back down to the row
of Mushroom Blocks, pick one up, climb the Mushroom Block Wall you built, and toss the Block at
Tryclyde. Do this with the remaining two Mushroom Blocks: score three direct hits and Tryclyde
will go bye, Clyde!

7/1: This is it: Wart's Castle! The first part, 7/1, is
going to be comparatively short and easy . . . something that is *not* true of the last world in the game,
7/2. Upon arriving, you'll find yourself on a Cloud.
Climb the Cloud steps to the Ladder, ascend, and
head right, ready to do battle with Albatosses, Bob-
Ombs, and Ninjis. Above all, be sure that you *stay
ahead of the Bob-Ombs*: when they explode, here,

they take sections of the stone Bridges with them, leaving nothing but the gaping holes and the ether ahead of you! You can perch atop the Columns to avoid their blasts, if need be. After the first stone Bridge, you'll come to the Mushroom-shaped roof of a house. The Grasses there all contain Vegetables. However, at the end of the next stone Bridge is a Column with Potion Grass on top; take it, go left, and work magic on the roof. Just do so with haste, or the Bob-Ombs will waste you. Recross the stone Bridge to the right, hop onto the Cloud, use the Mushroom Block as a cork to plug up the Jar ahead, and enter the house ahead. Avoiding the Sparks inside, get onto the top Ledge and grab the third Grass from the right: it's Potion! Enter Subspace here and reap the Mushrooms and Coins. Exit and get onto the roof, pulling the Vegetable there to bop any Shyguy who happens to be about. Then board an Albatoss for the long ride *left* . . . back to the beginning of the world. Go *past* the point where you started your trek, continuing left until you reach another Ladder. To the left of it is a Column, and beyond that a single Grass; yank it and a Rocket will appear . . . your only ticket out of this section.

When you land, you'll be in a horizontal Cloud region. Get the Cherries on the lower level, then double back a few paces and get onto the upper Cloud. Hop the Column ahead, then the one after that, and stop when you reach the next Column. Get the Cherries on top of the Column below you to the right, then fall in behind a Shyguy headed toward the Cherries below, at the base of the Column: follow him and you'll reach the goodies un-scathed. Get on top of the Column and head right to the Ladder. Hop up three Clouds—watching out for Sparks—and you'll find some Mushroom Blocks. Use these to bop Sparks, then stack them so you can reach the next Ladder with ease. Climb and, again, use the Mushroom Blocks to kill Sparks, then arrange the Blocks so you can get to the Cloud above. Climb one of the two central Ladders to the Ladder between them, then take either the Ladder on the left or right to reach the hut. Enter for your umpteenth battle with Birdo. Take the room's one Mushroom Block to the edge of Birdo's Ledge and clobber the creature; reclaim the Mushroom Block when you can and hit your foe two more times. The key to surviving here is to keep hopping to avoid being hit; don't hesitate to drop off the Ledge, if need be.

7/2: You've now reached the Castle proper, and things're about to get pretty interesting ... not to mention long, arduous, and challenging! To begin, go right along the Clouds and cross the drawbridge. Cross the thin catwalk inside, with an eye on the Shyguy Jar—you'll have to jump 'em; there are no weapons here! After the Jar, you'll come to another thin catwalk ... only this and successive walks all move! If that weren't bad enough, you have to fight Ninjis, Bob-Ombs, and Shyguys as you cross. Move *slowly* but don't stop; a steady rightward movement will get you through. When you reach the sole float-ing Block with a Chain hanging from it, you have a choice: whether to go down here or to continue to the end of this room and take a different route entirely. The two meet up eventually, but both offer different challenges. So that you can make an informed choice, we'll look at both routes.

Route One: Climb down the Chain. You'll end up in a vertical chamber whose floors are made entirely of Mushroom Blocks. Pick them up to give yourself access to the floors below ... and also to keep the Sparks at bay. Make sure you get all the Cherries in the room. The door at the bottom will take you to a horizontal room filled with hanging Chains and killer Sparks. Use the Chains like you used the Ladders back in 6/3, as a place to hang out (literally) until your enemies wander off. There are two doors in this room: both take you to different places. (You didn't think Wart would live in an easy-to-negotiate Castle, did you?) However, this time you'll want to enter both. The first door takes you to a secret chamber. The danger-free room contains Potion; use it and exit by the same door through which you entered. You'll be back in the horizontal Chain room; continue to the right, again watching out for Sparks. Enter the door in the room's far-right corner. Climb the Chain. Although the Chain will be broken in spots as you ascend in this vertical chamber, bridging the gaps is easy. Indeed, there's nothing too difficult about this room; if you stay on the Chain and don't veer slightly to either side, the Sparks won't touch you. If you decide to go for any of the Cherries that line the walls, do so speedily because *then* the Sparks will go after you!

The door at the top will lead you to a small, horizontal chamber with Sparks and Chains. You'll have to move fast, when the coast is clear, to go up the short Staircase to the left, past the second Chain and onto the third Chain. If you tarry, the Sparks'll get you. Climb the Chain to enter a large vertical room. Anything special here? You bet! Moving floors, populated by Shyguys, Sparks, and Snifits. Do *not* stay in one place for very long: the key to succeeding here is to keep moving upward in small leaps. Otherwise, you'll be overwhelmed. You should move straight up the center until you reach the Ledge below the Icicles, then go right. Climb steadily to the left until you reach the top of the Wall on that side, then study the four Ledges to the right to time your move. Once you clear these, it doesn't matter whether you go up to the left or right. The Chain overhead is your ticket out of here—and into the presence of the last Birdo. You can battle the bird or you can pass it—under or over—when it moves. Go up the Chain and head right at the top, past the Sparks, past the locked door, to the door beyond. Enter, and you'll find yourself where you *would* have been had you taken—

Route Two: Instead of climbing down the Chain, go right across the Catwalks to the Chain at the end of the room. When you reach the next room, go left and shimmy up the Chain that leads through the roof. (There's a room to the left, but don't worry

about that right now.) You're now in the bottom of
a large vertical chamber which is comprised of two
small rooms on the bottom and one large one above;
you must negotiate them using Chains and Ledges.
The Sparks in the lower two rooms of this section
won't trouble you much—treat them as you did the
Hoopsters on the Vines earlier, timing your shift
from Chain to Chain when the Sparks aren't near—
though the ones hovering around the first of the
blue Ledges requires a bit of patience: you must go
for the Chain on the left (there's a door you'll want
to enter), so wait until the coast is clear, then rush
ahead. Enter the door on the Ledge and you'll find
yourself outside the Castle. Climb down the series
of Ladders, pausing when necessary to avoid Panser's fire, or actually jumping off the Ladder and
falling down the right side, along the wall of the
Castle. Go into the door at the foot of the last Ladder, and you'll find yourself in that room we mentioned earlier. Get Potion from the Grass on the
right, enter Subspace, collect the Mushroom, and
head back through the door, up the Ladders, and
back into the Castle. When you've returned to the
vertical chamber with the Chains and Ledges, continue upward. One place to watch out for: the two
small Columns sitting on the last Ledge. Sparks
doggedly orbit that region as well as the Column
and Ledge to the lower left. Once you commit to
going through, do so *without stopping*, or you're
doomed. Climb the last Chain to the door on the
upper right. Be alert as you enter the door: there
are Sparks galore on the other side. Use the Chain

for sanctuary and the POW for offense, then head right. When you've climbed the next Chain, you'll be on a long Catwalk. Climb down the Chain at the end, descend using the Chain at the right, and you'll find yourself in a small room with a door. (This is the same place you'd have ended up if you'd taken *Route One*.) Enter, get the Key, and go to the locked door mentioned in *Route One*. Use the Key to enter. There are just two more rooms to clear.

The first room is a surprise: there *seems* to be no enemy here. However, when you near the Mask Door at the end, it won't open as usual: it will come off the wall and attack! Using the two Mushroom Blocks, score a total of three hits against the Mask and it will go back to where it belongs. Get the Crystal Ball and enter Wart's chamber. The big boss himself is sitting on the far-right side. He'll spit deadly Bubbles at you, while the Dream Machine in front of him ejects Vegetables. Your task: to catch the Vegetables and hit Wart when his mouth is open—but before he blows Bubbles. That's the only time he's vulnerable. When the chief villain has been fatally weakened, he'll change colors and expire.

And that frees Mario for his most complex and exciting adventure yet!

SUPER MARIO BROS. 3

Objective:

    Looks like there's never going to be a moment's rest for Mario. Bowser's back, intent on conquering the Mushroom World ... the realm beyond the Mushroom Kingdom. And *this* time Bowser's brought his putrid progeny, just to make things really unnerving. Specifically, the evildoers have stolen the Magic Wands from each nation of the Mushroom World and used them to transform each of the kings into beasts. (What? No queens? An enlightened place like the Mushroom World should *not* be chauvinistic!) Needless to say, Mario—or the Princess, Luigi, or Toad—must dare new dangers to defeat the villains and restore normalcy to the world.

Gameplay:

The most important innovations are the new powers that Mario et al. can acquire. By catching a power-up, Mario can become Raccoon Mario, able to fly and whack enemies with his tail. A Fire Flower transforms Mario into Fire Mario, able to throw fireballs. You also become Frog Mario during the course of the game and when surrounded by foes, can briefly become invincible—albeit immobile—Statue Mario if you're already Raccoon Mario. There are also the familiar Coins, Starman, 1-U-Mushrooms, and Super Mushrooms to acquire. As for the Blocks, there are Jump Blocks, ? Blocks as before, and Switch Blocks marked with a P which cause unpredictable results when touched. Other additions to the line-up include Toad's House, which allows Mario to pick up important tools, and the Spade Panel, in which additional Marios are awarded to players who correctly match rolling portions of a picture. Other items, such as Jugem's Cloud and Magic Wing, will be discussed where appropriate. The enemy characters are pictured and described in the instruction booklet, and will be mentioned in the *Strategies* section below as they crop up.

Points:

Points are awarded for virtually everything Mario does, from defeating enemies to collecting Coins and power-ups: 50 points for a Coin, 100 for bopping a Para-Goomba, and 1000 for nabbing a power-up.

Coins, Star
Bottom: Mushroom, Ten Coins, Star, Mushroom, Flower, Star

Now . . . let's boogie!

Grass Land

1/1: World One is going to be a cinch for experi-
enced Marioers. Scroll the screen left as little as
possible until you've gotten the Mushroom from the
fourth? (the other ?'s are Coins). The first Pipe contains a fireball-spitting Venus Fire Trap; leap over
it between the blasts and hunker down on the right
side of the pipe. The plant can't get you there.
(When you get good, you can actually leap over the
Venus Fire Trap and get past it before it can fire!)
Continue right, hopping over the green and orange
Walls, killing the Turtlelike Koopa by leaping on
it from the left—and hopping back to the left after
you bash it. Kick the Shell into the next ? to release
the power-up, and go collect it before it falls off the
bottom of the screen. Get the Coin from the ? then
prepare to deal with the Goombas and a Para-
Goomba—which has wings and must be bopped
twice—on the long stretch just ahead. Clobber them
all, then head back to the left—to the power-up
Block—accelerate, and take to the skies flying diagonally to the upper right, following the string of
Coins and, natch, collecting them all. (For begin-
ners, it's best to build up speed thusly. Put the con-

troller on a flat surface. With one hand, hold the
pad down and keep the B button pressed in, while
with the other hand push the A button.) On the
first set of Jugem's Clouds, bump the glowing Block
overhead, then scoot up on the right side of the
Block to collect the Mushroom. Continue right,
gathering all the Coins, then do *not* descend; fly to
the right until you reach the Pipe, and go down. It
will take you to a Coin room. When you emerge,
you'll be just a few hops from the end of the level. (If
you didn't enter the Pipe but dropped down, you'll
land on a stack of glowing Blocks: bop the Koopa
and use the Shell to smash them. You'll uncover a
Switch Block here—top right of the bunch on the
left. By the way: as in other Mario games, make
sure you don't get nailed if the Shell hits an im-
passe and rebounds!) If possible, try to freeze the
timer at the end of the round with the clock show-
ing an even number and the Coin and point count
each being a multiple of eleven.

1/2: The first ? in the new realm contains a power-
up, just in case you got demoted from Super Mario!
Even if you didn't, get it: it's worth 1000 points.
Watch out for the Para-Goombas after the Pipe.
Now, this part's important. Go to the right side of
the T-shaped Pipe. Goombas will begin pouring out.
If you can crush nine of them, *without* touching the
ground, you'll get a 1-Up—plus all the points you
accumulated for mashing the little guys. Keep
stomping Goombas after that: you'll get an additional 1-Up for *every one you bop*! Stay here as long

as you want, collecting 1-Ups. When you continue
to the right and reach the floating Coins with the
Pipe and Venus Fire Trap, collect the Coins only if
you can fly. Otherwise, don't. Go past them, to the
right, and hit the left Block of the Ledge *closest* to
the ground, underneath the Pipe. It's a Switch
Block and will turn the Coins to Blocks. You can
use the Blocks to climb to the pipe, get a 1-Up
Mushroom above and to the right of it, then slide
down the Pipe and enter a Coin room. Even better,
when you emerge you'll be at the Pipe *before* the
one you entered, allowing you to collect the Coins
now instead of turning them into Blocks. A few
easy-to-beat Goomba-types will attack, after which
you'll reach a pair of Jump Blocks; there's a power-
up in the one on the right. Continue to the next
Pipe, sliding down the hill and crouching on the left
side of the Pipe—to avoid the Venus Fire Trap.
When the plant retreats, hop over and continue:
you'll run into three Jump Blocks, the third of
which contains a Starman. The last ? is a Coin; the
end of the round is just beyond.

1/3: Stomp the first Koopa you see, pick up its Shell,
and sling it at the next foe that attacks you; the
Shell will continue beyond and smash a few of the
Blocks ahead. When you arrive, squash the red
Koopa and use its Shell to obliterate the Blocks;
when you've cleared a path so you can stand at the
right of the ? (which contains a power-up), leap
straight up. You'll uncover an invisible Jump
Block. Hop on and it'll vault you into the strato-

sphere. There, you can collect mucho Coins and a
1-Up Mushroom without an enemy in sight! Descend the Pipe and you'll be deposited at the end of
the level. If you decided to stay on the ground, you
can collect Coins there—though not nearly as many
as above. However, there *is* one enormous benefit
to staying on the ground. If you stand on the white
Wall above the foliage—the third Block from the
left—and squat in the center, you'll fall *through* the
Wall and end up in a hidden Toad House where
you'll find a Magic Whistle. If you blow it now, you
can warp ahead to World Two, Three, or Four. It's
better, however, to save it and use it when you've
found the other Whistles.

1/4: This is a realm of Ledges and floating Logs. Be
careful when you use the latter: they're extremely
useful, but dangerous in that they drift over and
then drop suddenly. Make sure you're not on it
when it does so, or it's kaput time! After you leave
the *third* Log, you'll come to a short Ledge with a
smaller one beneath it, the two of them flush on
the right. If you're good, you can jump up against
the upper Ledge from the Log. If you're still learning the ropes, get on the lower Ledge, jump up
against the upper Ledge, and you'll uncover a
Mushroom in the second Block from the right. Grab
it quickly, or it'll fall away. Continue to the right:
hit the leftmost Block of the Ledge that has a
prowling Koopa—the fiend is red—and you'll get
multiple Coins. Bop Koopa—or, if you time it right,
you can slay the Turtle simply by hitting up on the

Coin Block when the creature is just to the right of it—pick up its Shell, ride the next Log, and throw the Shell against the lone Block standing on the right of the Ledge on top. You'll get another Mushroom. When you come to the vertical string of Coins, hop on the Log and ride it down to collect them ... jumping off to the right, onto the *top* of the L-shaped Ledge. Jump up against the Block above and you'll get multiple Coins. You'll reach a Pipe in a few moments, and it'll take you to the end of the level. You'll be able to play match the cards now: do a good job and you can get five extra Marios! Note: if you accumulate at least 44 Coins in this level, you'll be allowed to enter the White House on the map screen. There, you'll be able to acquire a P-Wing.

World One Fortress: after leaping three pits, hit the first ? for a power-up. When you enter the corridor ahead, wafflelike foes called Rotodiscs will attack from the ceiling. These move in a clockwise direction—except for the first, which orbits counterclockwise. If you're Raccoon Mario, fly over these foes altogether; if not, after you get through the corridor and leap three pits, make sure you hit the next ? for a power-up. Immediately after the ? you'll encounter Dry Bones for the first time. Right after you beat the mummified Turtle, go to the far right *without* entering the door. Hold down the B button and accelerate, running to the left: fly up, go over the Wall (heading right) and continue traveling right, along the top of the Wall, until you reach a room. There, you'll find the second Whistle, which you should add to your arsenal instead of using it. Go to the map and continue your quest. If you didn't take this route, then after you kill Dry Bones, enter the door beyond the dusty tortoise, and the ceiling will come down to crush you. No problem—as long as you make sure that when it does, you snuggle into one of the little alcoves in the ceiling. Even though there are Spikes in these, you'll be safe. (Note: if you rush ahead when the ceiling starts to descend, you'll be able to reach the second—and last—alcove in one spring. You *can* make it, and you'll be in an ideal position to enter the next door when the ceiling rises.) That next door takes you to the mini-boss Boom Boom; as soon as you spot him, run over, jump on the creature's head three times, and it's bye bye Boom Boom.

1/5: This is an ice realm, and you begin by sliding down an incline and demolishing the Buzzy Beetles waiting for you. After you somersault over the Pit—collecting the Coins as you go—watch out for the downward-facing Pipe: a deadly plant waits within. Once past this, you can go one of two ways: along the upper corridor, or to the right of the Pipe below. If you take the high road, you'll find an invisible Jump Block at the top left of the corridor. Leap on it and you'll be catapulted to Clouds filled with Coins. Make sure that you fly *over* the layer of Coins close to the Clouds: there's another level higher up, along with a Block containing a 1-Up Mushroom. The Pipe will return you to the surface more than halfway through the realm. If you took the low road, watch out for the killer plant in the first Tube. Beyond it, you'll find Coins—jump in the water and hop up and down to get the moolah—and, at the end (before the corridor slopes up), you'll get a Flower from the ?. You'll emerge at the same place from which the Pipe would've dropped you if you'd gone into the Clouds. Climb the ice steps, slide down the slope, nail the Koopa, then go down the Pit *carefully* or you'll slip right into the waiting maw of the Venus Fire Trap that lives in the first Pipe. (You can also use the slain Koopa to bop the Flower.) The first downward-facing Pipe also contains a deadly plant. When you get past it and re-emerge on the surface, the round will be over. (Note: if you start running just to the left of the jagged line that separates the sky from the black, and jump at the Card, you'll almost always get a Star.)

1/6: There's an interesting new gadget on this level: Logs that ride along on wire tracks, colloquially known as Rail Lifts. When you begin, a Koopa first appears on the Log with the floating Coins. Bop it and toss its Shell down to the right to destroy the Koopa on the Log below. Get the power-up from the ? above that Log. Continue right: you'll pass a green nub atop a Log, two Jump Blocks, a green Hill on a Log beyond them and, a bit farther, a green Hill with two small vertical Walls of Blocks and a Ledge above it—as well as a Koopa between them. Kill the Koopa, use its Shell to bash its winged companion to the left, then bust up the Blocks overhead: the second Block from the right contains a 1-Up Mushroom. Hop on the first Log suspended by blue cables; at the end, get on the skinny Log and start running, continuing across the next cable-supported Log: it's difficult, but you should be able to get enough speed going to fly up to get the floating Coins. If not, drop down to the sole Block at the end of the first cable-supported Log and get on the wire-guided Log to the right. The former tack, obviously, will get you more Coins. If you are able to fly, follow the Coins downward until you land on the Log below the last group. The wire-pulled Log will leave you off here as well. (If you take the wire-driven Log, watch out for the winged Turtle that will drop down on you.) From here, it's an easy few hops to the end of the level. (Beware: there's a Koopa waiting for you beneath the Card! Be sure you jump a little earlier than usual.)

World One Ship: it's time to do battle on the first of the Koopa Ships you'll encounter. First, though, congrats to the programmer who came up with the ominous drumbeat that opens this round. It's super! Before you begin, here's a sorry bit of news: your fireballs are useless on the boat. Speed and agility are your primary "weapons." However, they're not your only weapon: if you stand on the top of a cannon, your feet just overhanging the mouth, the Bullet Bills that come out won't hurt you *and* you'll get 100 points for each one you stop in this fashion. To begin your crossing, no sooner do you board the ship than Cannons begin firing at you. Pass the first one and stand directly behind it until the second one has fired, then run ahead and

get behind—to the right of—that one. Duck: a third
Cannon, firing horizontally instead of diagonally
like the first two, will take Mario's head off if you
don't! What's more, this Cannon fires in both directions, so *don't* stand behind it; instead, jump down
to the next platform—you can't miss it: there's another diagonally-firing Cannon to the right—and
hug the Wall on the left. When the diagonally-firing
Cannon has fired, jump it and continue to the right.
Cross that small Wall quickly: not only will the
horizontally-firing Cannon be shooting, still, but
there's a diagonally-shooting Cannon in the upper
right firing down at that very Wall. Cross the deck
to the next thin Wall—with a horizontally-shooting
Cannon on it. There's a diagonally-shooting Cannon above it to the right; hop on the Cannon on the
Wall when it and the one above have just fired.
When you're on the other side, you're safe until you
reach the ? Block. There's a Flower in there, and
you should get it . . . but don't dally. Above, to the
right, is a Cannon that not only fires in *four* directions, it rotates to make sure one gun is always
trained on you! Hop the Wall in front of you and
rush ahead, and you'll be safe. After a short section
of deck, you'll see another diagonally-shooting Cannon aimed to the upper right. Slip into the alcove
behind it. When the Cannon has fired, hop over it
and run forward. The horizontally-firing Cannon in
front of you won't touch you if you stay on the
ground. Hop it and hug the right side of the Wall
it's on; when it and the diagonally-shooting Cannon
to its right have fired, rush up the Staircase. (You

can leap the Wall and run up the steps in one un-
broken sprint . . . but that's only advised for expe-
rienced players.) Enter the Pipe on the top of the
Staircase and you'll do battle with the first of Bowser's kids: Larry. He'll throw Smoke Rings at you,
but these are easy to dodge. All you have to do is
jump on his head three times—when he's out of his
Shell—and he's a goner. The Wand is yours, and
one king has been restored!

Desert Land

2/1: Upon entering this arid, sandy world, get under the first ? Block and wait. You'll be faced with
hopping Blocks known as Pile Driver Micro-
Goombas on this level. These are apparently stable
Blocks that suddenly leap at you from the side. A
Block will hop at you from the right; when it's right
above the ? Block, jump up and hit the ? That'll
release a power-up *and* smash the incoming Micro-
Goomba. There's another Micro-Goomba just to the
right of where the last one took off—the top Block
at the end of the next section of Blocks—so jump on
it before it can launch itself. You'll find nothing in
any Blocks until you reach the small two-Block horizontal Ledge of ?'s after the three vertical Walls.
(Note: there are Micros atop each Wall, so fly over
if you're Raccoon Mario.) The rightmost ? contains
a Starman. Bash the Koopa below and, if you
missed the Starman, use the Turtle's Shell to smash
the Micro to the right. Beware the Fire Snake just

before the third Micro—which, when smashed, will
give you a power-up. Use the Jumping Blocks that
follow and vault up to the "runway" ahead. Kill
the Goombas, then drop off the right side of the
runway, bop the Block on the left, collect the power-
up, hit the empty space to the right of that Block
to uncover an invisible Jumping Block, then go left,
under the runway, and break the underside. Go inside and collect the Coins and a Mushroom from the
lone Block. (You can avoid the Fire Snake in there
by bopping the Block, then tucking yourself into
the left corner below it and wait for the Mushroom
to reach you. The snake can't get you here.) Hop
onto the Ledge to the left, break through the runway to the top, go right to the edge, then run left
and fly up to the floating Pipe, which you can enter
by shattering the Blocks around it with your tail.
The Switch Block inside will reveal a load of Coins.
When you drop from the Coin room, you'll be on
another runway with Blocks and a Fire Snake inside. Break the last Block on the top, run to the
right to the next Pipe, then run back and the Blocks
will all be Coins. Break in using the Block on the
lower right, wait patiently for the Fire Snake to
come out, jump in and collect the Coins, then exit
using the Block on the upper left—that way, the
Fire Snake won't get you. Return to the Pipe on
the right, go to the one beyond it, and enter when
the killer Flower descends. (It's also suggested that
you return to the Pipe up above: you can collect the
Coins all over again!) After doing the Switch Block

routine and clearing the Coins from this room, you
will have completed the level.

2/2: This level will gift you with a visit to the White
Mushroom House if you collect at least 30 Coins.
That *includes* all the Blocks that can become Coins
when you use the Switch Block. To begin: bop the
Goomba, get past the killer plant, and hit the first
Block for a power-up. There's another plant after
the pipe, and a sea after the first Wall. If you've got
Raccoon power, you can ride the Log and then fly;
if not, you'll have to go for a dip at some point. Flying, you'll be dealing with your winged Turtle pals;
swimming, it's killer fish whose touch is deadly. Incidentally—if you're good, you can stay in the air
even if you're not Raccoonized. Simply bounce off
the backs of the airborne Koopas as you go along!
Anyway—go through the level and collect all the
visible Coins, then go back to the left and get on the
Log. As you cross the lake again, hit the right Block
of the first Ledge; it's a Switch Block. Quickly
gather all the Coins that were Blocks so you can get
to the White Mushroom room. The Pipe at the end
takes you out of this level and to—

World Two Fortress: your new foes here are the
Thwomps, big ugly-faced Blocks that crush whatever gets beneath them, rise, then get set to come
down again. These granite guys cannot be stopped
or destroyed. However, when they come down, you
can jump on top of and over them. The first appears
right after the initial trio of mummy Turtles. If you
keep stomping these Dry Bones as you did the Goom-

bas in 1/2—that is, without touching the ground—
you can earn more 1-Ups as before. The second
Thwomp comes after the next herd of Turtles—
Turtle herdle? Immediately after you face the second Thwomp, the first Boo Diddly appears in the
upper left corner. You can wait until it comes down
low enough for you to jump on it, or simply race
ahead, bopping the Dry Bones as you pass. Enter
the Pipe at the far side of the room. When you
emerge, you'll have to cross a Spike Pit; no problem, you say—except that there's a Thwomp ready
to fall on the landing in the middle of the Pit. You
can make it across, though, if you race ahead without pausing on that Ledge. When you reach the
other side of the Spikes, hit the right Block of the
Ledge—below the second Boo Diddly: you'll get a
power-up. Then race like the wind to get past the
four Thwomps that fall in quick succession. You
can get through using a stop-and-go technique, but
there's no reason for caution here when speed will
do the trick! Enter the door at the end and you'll
be in a room whose Ledges are lined with Spikes
and come down toward the floor. These are best
taken using stop-and-go. Just don't stop anywhere
for *too* long, or the Boo Diddlies will come down and
get you. Upon entering the last chamber, you've got
to battle the Boom Boom Koopa. Jump on its head
three times to destroy it; just don't do so when its
porcupinelike quills are extended, or you'll perish.

2/3: Welcoming you to the next level is a Fire
Snake. Just go to the right until it scrolls off the

screen, then return to the left and it'll be gone. Get rid of the Koopa on the Pyramid and use its Shell to break the Block beneath the ? on the right. Then get under the ? Block and hit it for a power-up. The next Pyramid has a Starman in the ? on the right. The third Pyramid will give you a power-up—a Super Leaf if you got the Mushroom at the first Pyramid—in the left ? Block. Beware the Micro atop the next Pyramid, and those jumping over from the twin Pyramid beside it. Go to the Block to the left of the Pyramid on the right, and hop up to the right using the two Jump Blocks. These will take you to a Ledge; fly from it to the upper left and you'll find two small Ledges, one atop the other. The upper Ledge contains a Switch Block, which will turn the Pyramids below into a slew of Coins! Dropping down and collecting them, you'll have no trouble getting the 1-Up in the middle of the left Pyramid. If you can't get up to the Switch Block for some reason, kill the Koopas here and use their Shells to smash the Pyramid on the left; fifth row from the bottom, second Block from the right, contains the 1-Up Mushroom. The next (and last) structure is really a half Pyramid. When you arrive, smack all the Blocks that comprise the Staircase on the left: you'll get a Coin from each. Then go to the edge of the top step, overlooking the Pit on the right. Jump on top of one Koopa, then hop back up to the step *pronto*. Toss the Shell down and it'll smash the Blocks covering the Pipe. Before you enter the Pipe, get under the Block to the left, equal with the opening: hit it for multiple Coins.

World Two Desert: this is a relatively simple realm. After you pass the Venus Fire Traps, grab the Shell of the first Koopa you meet and carry it with you. When you meet the Whirlwind, jump right into its eye and let it cart you ahead. When you emerge, the Sun will try to set on you, chasing you around and giving new meaning to the word "sunburn." To protect yourself, use the Koopa Shell to smash the stellar pain in the neck.

2/4: To get the first ? Block, kill one of the Koopas—on the left or right Wall—and ricochet the Shell down against the ? Block. Jump down and claim the power-up. A little farther along is another Koopa: bop it and use the Shell to smack open the next ? and get another power-up. You should certainly have Raccoon Mario by now, which is important: most of the goodies in this level are located above. More on that in a moment. A Boomerang Brother is ahead, and in case you've been hit there's another power-up in the next ? Block—to the left of the Pipe with the killer Plant. When you reach the jagged line of demarcation at the end of the level, turn and fly to the *left*, following the Jumping Blocks—the lowest of which has a power-up. When you've reached the land in the sky, hit the second Block to the upper left to uncover a Switch Block. When you've gotten the Coins, go all the way to the lake on the left: stay on the right side of the Ledge above the water and hit the third Block from the left—another Switch Block is here. Collect the Coins, then head back to the right and exit . . . but watch it! A Boomerang Brother is waiting for you below the Card. (Note: if you can get to the Card before he throws, you'll be rewarded with a Coin *and* 1000 points when the killer evaporates!) However, the most important thing to remember about this level is none of the above! What's important? The fact that you can get the third Magic Whistle after winning here . . . and, having gotten it, you can use the three Whistles to warp to World Eight! Go and battle the Hammer Brother wandering near here, beat him, get the Hammer, and return to the Map. Using the weapon, you can continue to the right—even though the Map *seems* to end—where you'll do battle with another Turtle; one of the Fire Brothers. Kill him, and you'll get the last Whistle. Now, use the Whistles to their limit! Obviously, there is *one* serious disadvantage to taking a shortcut like this. You won't have the weapon you'll need to make a dent in World Eight. Still, there's no sense being faint-hearted: give it a try!

2/5: It's new foe time. This level introduces Chain Chomp, the carnivorous ball-and-chain. Beware: though the monster is fettered, the chain will break after 160 timer-seconds have passed. So don't stand around staring at the creature. Get the power-up in the ? on the right only when the Chain Chomp is chomping in another direction . . . or slay it using the Shell of the Koopa roaming to the right. The next power-up is just beyond Chain Chomp number two, in the Block on the ground, to the right of the Chomp's Block. You can snuggle under the Ledge to the right to get it, or kick it from the left when the Chomp is at rest. But hop on the Block quickly after you kick it, or the power-up will float away. As you cross the Wall to the right, you'll pass a water Pit and, after that, two Koopas: kill the one on top and throw its Shell against the sole Block to the right, beside a section of Wall, for a Coin. Now, just beyond that is a narrow Pit with a Ledge to the right and a second Pit beyond it. Bop the Koopa to the right of the second Pit, and carry the Shell back to the Pit on the left—the one just below the section of Wall where you got the Coin. It'll start smashing Blocks; when it hits the lowest Block on the left, a Vine will sprout. Climb it for floating Coins hidden above the Clouds, then enter the Pipe on the left side of this Coin heaven. Upon descending, bop the Block on the bottom right for a power-up, then hit the block directly *above* the one Block on the bottom, center. This is a Switch Block, and will turn all the Blocks to Coins. When you emerge from the Pipe, you'll be on a Wall in the sky: all of the ? Blocks contain Coins, save for the last one on the right, which will give you a power-up. Descend and exit the level. Since there are no foes under the Card, you can take a running leap at it to get a Star.

World Two Pyramid: this is a good place to be if you're just plain ol' Mario. If you enter the Pyramid, get a power-up, exit, and reenter: you can get the power-up again. The object in question is lo-

cated in the overhanging Block of the first Wall you
encounter. Just bash the two Buzzies that get in
your way, slide down the ramp, and jump up to the
Ledge on your right. Smash the Wall up ahead of
you, go past the Pipe with the Venus Fire Trap inside, and head up to the Ledge on the left. Go left.
At the Wall, jump up to the right. Shatter the Wall
ahead of you, pass under the Ledge, jump up to the
right of the Wall to uncover an Invisible Block, then
get on it and leap over the Wall so you can enter
the Pipe. Taking care not to shatter any Blocks unless it's necessary, collect the Coins, get the 1-Up
by jumping at the fifth Block from the right, on top.
Then hit the lone Block on the bottom. Activate the
Switch Block to turn the remaining Blocks into
Coins. When you leave, you'll emerge from the Pipe
to find a pair of Buzzies sliding down at you from
the left. Run quickly up the slope on the right, then
continue right, along the corridor . . . watching out
for the Buzzies, who not only attack on the ground,
but also crawl along the ceiling and drop down on
you! Fortunately, you can use their Shells to bowl
down others and to smack apart the Wall up ahead.
Watch out for the killer plant in the Pipe just before the Exit Pipe, and be prepared to battle the
Boomerang Brother who will be waiting for you as
soon as you leave the Pipe—not below the Cards, as
in most previous rounds.

World Two Ship: the not-so-warm welcome here
consists of two Cannons firing at you, one low and
one high; they fire in reverse as well, so don't think
you'll be safe by simply hopping over the first. You

must get on top of the taller one and go from there to the upper deck. Naturally, things aren't going to be much fun up there; you'll take just a few steps and find yourself assaulted by a Cannon mounted on the side of the deck, firing diagonally to the upper right. That's easy enough to scoot past, but don't get overly confident: when you reach the end of the deck, make sure you drop down on top of the horizontally-firing Cannon down there, which hasn't quite scrolled onto the screen from the right yet—just jump as if it were there, and it'll scroll under you. If you land on the deck proper, that Cannon will perforate you. Leap off that Cannon to the Cannon on the deck below, to the right. Get off of it to the right, and hurry to the low Cannon there between shots. When you hop up to the deck on the right, make sure you do so immediately after a Bullet Bill has already come at you from the left. The ? on the new deck contains a Flower.

Jump down to the Crates and drop down the first gap between them, to the right, then head to the right—not the left, where the Cannons are. Waiting until a volley of Bullet Bills passes you by, drop down to the deck along the left side of the Mast. Negotiate this little zig zag course *without stopping*, or the Cannons will blast you to pulsating little particles. Hurry under the Mast and get on the Crate to its right. Go to the top of the Crates *fast* or the Cannons on the right will end your seafaring days. Continue along the Crate tops to the next deck on the right. Bop the "lids" of the Rocky Wrenches before they can rise from the deck and throw Wrenches at you, then jump on top of the second of the two Cannons ahead—like the one before, it's the taller of the two. If you get on the first one, the second will kill you. Enter the Pipe beyond to battle Morton Koopa Jr. Wait until he goes into the little Pit beside his perch, then jump on him once. Go to the right—to his perch—and circle him clockwise when he jumps up at you, dropping down on his head when you're at the twelve o'clock position. Repeat the orbit and hit him one more time: three strikes and he's out. However, he's only vulnerable when he's outside of his Shell.

Water Land

3/1: It's bathing suit time, folks. Drop into the water and go straight down: you'll get a power-up in the ? under the big Sea Ledge. Swim left and up, then head right. You'll pass four upward-facing Pipes and will eventually reach a set of ?'s with a Flower on the left and a Coin on the right. When the Lava Lotus is still, pass under them from the left to right, bopping both. Then go back to the left to collect the Flower. Go up to the right of the Pipe overhead. Swim to the top of the water and use your jumping power to get on top of the Wall on the left. Cross to the left, drop into the little Pond up there, and collect the power-up from the ? Retrace your steps to the right and dive back into the sea. Swim over the three stalks of coral, then dive down to the section filled with Jump Blocks. Beyond them, to

the right, is a Block with a 1-Up Mushroom, surrounded by Coins. Be careful when you dogpaddle
up under the Block and bop it: if you're not quick,
the Mushroom will scurry away and fall, irretriev-
ably, into the Pit below. When you've got it, go to
the Pipe on the right and ride the current up to the
downward-facing Pipe above. Exit the level.

3/2: It's more Rail Lifts to start, though they move
faster than their predecessors. After you cross the
first two Rail Lifts—you can actually skip the second one by leaping over it—you'll reach a row of
Blocks (a Donut Lift) with a ? on the right. Just
stand on the Blocks and they'll fall, enabling you
to get under the ? for a Flower. Ride the next Rail
Log, shooting the leaping Cheep-Cheeps below
you—or jumping up and landing on them if you
don't have fireball power. Almost at once you'll be
passing under a Ledge with a lone Block on the left
side: get off and make absolutely certain that you
get the Starman in that Block. Not only will you become invincible, but there's a surprise, which we'll
tell you about in a second. Pass under the next ?
while riding the Rail Lift, and knock the Coins from
it. Now, when you pass under the next ?, you'll get
Coins . . . *unless* you got the Starman. If you did,
then you'll get another Starman here . . . and a
third Starman from the next ? you encounter, immediately after leaving the Lift. (If you didn't get
the first Starman, then the new ? will just be Coins
too.) Get on the second Rail Lift; while you travel
as before, watch out for the winged Koopa that de-

scends. (Note: don't use its Shell to shatter the
Blocks ahead. You'll want the Blocks intact!) When
you pass under the Ledge, hit the third Block from
the left: it's a Switch Block. Beyond it, to the left
of the Pipe, is an Invisible Block that contains a
1-Up. When you reach the Pipe, blast the plant inside
and go to the right, hop in the water, and bop the
? for a Flower. When that's done, get on it and hit
the unmarked Block above to get a Coin. When
you're finished, enter the Pipe and you'll be
whisked to the end of the level. However, it's not
quite time to leave: if you're Raccoon Mario, fly up,
board the Rail Lift in the sky, and collect more
Coins and a 1-Up before departing 3/1.

3/3: Just go leaping from Ledge to Ledge at the
start, keeping an eye on the water, which will be
rising—or are the Ledges sinking? Fish large and
small will be jumping up at you. When you reach
the long row of Blocks, hit the Jump Block and a
Flower will emerge beneath it. The most spectacu-
lar way to get to the Flower is to bop the Koopa to
the right and carry its Shell ahead to the dip in the
Ledge. Throw the Shell to the left, smashing the
Blocks so you can get to the Flower. The drawback
to this tactic is that it'll smash a Switch Block—the
second Block from the right in the same line as the
Jump Block. So, obviously, you'd be wiser to hit
the Jump Block, activate the Switch Block, and
then methodically collect the Coins and power-up.
Continue to the right, using the Rotary Lift ahead
by jumping on the green fulcrum when the Lift

stops spinning. On the Ledge beyond, the top Block will give you a Flower; the one to the left is a Switch Block. (If you don't have Raccoon power, simply pick up a Block on the right and throw it at the Switch Block. By the way—these Blocks can also be used to fight the fish!) There's not much else you need to know about this level. Until you reach the Pipe, the only obstacles hereafter are the rising and falling islands and the leaping fish. When you reach the Pipe, go past it and you'll get a 1-Up Mushroom from the lone glowing Block. Return to the Pipe, enter, and say good-bye to the sea!

World Three Fortress: you'll experience an unhappy sense of déjà vu here! In just one short corridor you have to deal with some old nemeses: two Rotodiscs with a Dry Bones between them, a Thwomp, and another Dry Bones. Leap the first Rotodisc when it's at the four o'clock position, land on Dry Bones as you're coming down, then just shuffle past the next disc. It's more of the same as you continue down the hallway. Now, there're two things you can do to warp right to Boom Boom. First, you can enter the third door in the corridor and quickly press up; this will whisk you right to the Boom Boom room. Or you can enter the *sixth* door. When you go through, head up to the left and enter the first door you come to. This, too, will take you right to Boom Boom. Of course, if you're daring and go to the very end of the corridor, you'll be rewarded with a Coin room. When you enter, make sure you uncover the Invisible Block right over the doorway, or else you won't be able to collect all the riches!

Also, if you're powered-down, you can replenish
yourself by going in the *second* door. You'll fall into
a sewer; swim to the left and get the power-up in
the ? there, then swim to the right and get the next
power-up in another ? You're now Raccoon Mario.
(Swim all the way to the right and, to the left of
the last door, you'll notice a Block with a 1-Up. To
get to this, try the doors back in the corridor!) You
can exit the sewer via the downward-opening Pipe—
which will take you back to the main corridor, right
under the first Thwomp—or you can go to the steps
midway between the two ? Blocks, enter the door
at the *top* of the staircase—not the one on the bottom—and you'll be in Boom Boom's room. When you
face the boss, you'll have to suppress a yawn: three
quick bops and he's chopped liver.

3/4: Wimpy Goombas start things off here, along
with Venus Fire Traps in a pair of Pipes. Hug the
side of the Pipe until the plants stop firing, then
proceed. The ? to the right of the second Pipe is a
power-up. Slide down the hill and cut down the
Goombas there, then land in the water; jump up on
the right side, just above the waterline, and you'll
reveal an Invisible Block with a Coin. Get on top
of it and jump to the upper left to reveal a second
Invisible Block and Coin, then go to the cliff on the
right. Mow down the Koopas on the Hill, then bop
the ?'s on the other side for Coins. When you reach
the downward-facing Pipe, a not-sorely-missed enemy from another game returns: the Lakitu, dropping Spinys on you. Stay on the Ledge of glowing

Blocks and jump on top of the annoying creature when you can. Or there's something else you can do: get a slew of 1-Ups. Remember those Koopas you chopped down a moment ago? When you do that, take the Shell of one of them and go to the two-? Ledge beneath the Pipe—killing the plant within, if you have fireball power. When Lakitu arrives, toss the Shell down so that it shuttles back and forth between the two Blocks on the ground. The Spinys will land in the Shell's path: each time the Shell hits one, you'll get an extra Mario. When you've had your fill, get a Flower from the ? to the right of the Pipe, then activate the Switch Block on the right side of the Ledge below the Pipe. A new Lakitu will arrive in a moment, and you have a few options here. You can get on the next Ledge of ?'s— there's a Coin in the left ?, a power-up in the right— and jump on your foe, or you can race ahead to the end of the round: there's nothing in your way and, though the flying nightmare will flit ahead of you, you'll easily reach the Card before any Spinys are dropped. Lakitu perishes when you get the Card.

3/5: Jelectros try to sizzle you in the sea realm that follows. Since they can't be harmed, give them a wide berth! Moreover, if you have a Frog suit, it's suggested that you use it here! First, if you're Raccoon Mario, stay on top of the water and mount the island to the right. You'll find ten Coins on top. Dive off the island to the left, and go down to the left to get the Coins. Head right, under the L-shaped Ledge: the leftmost of the three ?'s will give you a

Flower, the others will spit out Coins. Make sure you also tap the Blocks to the right of the ? Blocks for Coins. As you perform all this derring-do, make sure you keep an out out for the Cheep-Cheeps, which will be swimming your way. Head right along the bottom of the screen for Coins, then go straight down when you reach the downward-facing Pipe: there are more Coins to be had. Swim under the Ledge with the six sea rocks stacked like a right triangle, and, if you're wearing the Frog Suit, you can get into the Pipe; if not, forget it. Inside, you'll be rewarded with Coins *and* 1-Ups. If you couldn't get in, continue right, hit the row of three ?'s—there are Coins left and right, and a power-up in the center—then go up and over the two Walls. You're at a long downward-facing Pipe: hit up under it, slightly to the right, to uncover an Invisible Block with a 1-Up Mushroom. Continue past the schools of sea life and under the island; when you clear the land mass, swim to the upper right and the surface. Jump up to the island—which should be on your left—and collect the ten Coins on top. Dive back in on the right side, go straight down for the Coins atop the squat wall, then swim to the right. When you reach the horizontal Pipe, enter . . . and exit!

3/6: Time for another Lift level. Get on and off the Donut Lifts in a hurry, though not so fast that you fail to get the power-up from the first ?. Hit the Block from below, get on the solid Log Ledge to the right, then collect your reward. Cross the Rotary Lift to the Donut Lift beyond, and watch out for the

Koopa marching along the Ledge on the right. Kick the creature so that its Shell goes to the right: it'll fall and gather the ten Coins located below. At the end of the next Ledge, jump off onto the back of the flying Koopa and hop left to get onto the Ledge below: the Block there has a power-up. Break the Block overhead to get back to the upper Ledge and hop from Ledge to Ledge. When you come to the two parallel Ledges, get on the lower Ledge, take one of the Blocks and throw it to the right. It'll trigger a Switch Block. Also make sure you jump up and unleash the 1-Up Mushroom, directly overhead; hit the Block on the left side so the Mushroom will roll to the right, allowing you to nab it when it drops through the Coins. Head right to the Rotary Lift and the Exit Pipe.

3/7: The welcoming committee on this level consists of Spike, a little green punk who throws Spiked Balls at you. Though the Balls are deadly, all you have to do is avoid them and bash Spike as you would a Koopa. (Regular Mario doesn't have to do a thing to avoid them: they pass right over his head.) When you begin, get on the Wall and hit the ? for a Coin, then hit the Wall itself for a power-up. Head right. The block of Blocks overhead contains a 1-Up, after which there's nothing much doing until you pass the Pipe. The Block on the ground contains a Flower. Climb the green Hill and get onto the *lower* Ledge to its right. Jump up beneath the *left* side of the Ledge overhead and a Vine will sprout. Climb it to the Coins in the sky. If you go all the way to the left, you'll find a Switch Block that will turn the block of Blocks back on the ground into Coins. When you leap back down (off the right), don't go all the way to the ground. Rather, land on the Clouds, hop onto the Jump Block and vault to a second Coin heaven. Back on the ground, at the end of the level, the second Block on the blue staircase contains a power-up.

World Three Fortress: ah ... more water. Nothing much to say about this place except that the only ? contains a power-up, and there are swarms of Cheep-Cheeps to deal with. In the first chamber, stay at the top and you'll be able to slip past the two Rotodiscs; in the next room, just go where the Stretches aren't. At the end, you'll face a spiked Boom Boom, easily beaten when its quills are withdrawn.

3/8: You'll have a Vine time on this level, but whatever you do, make sure you get 44 Coins so you can get to the White Mushroom House. Hit the first Block you encounter—with your Raccoon tail or, if you don't have one, with a Koopa or another Block—and a Vine will grow. Use it as a perch to escape the floodwaters. (Don't miss the Jump Block while you're up there: it'll give you a power-up.) You'll get the multiple Coins from the top Block on the stack of Blocks farther on, and a 1-Up from the Block under the Coins—use a Koopa to access it. The next Block contains another Vine, as does the next *single* Block after that—there's a two-Block slab between them. When you reach the rising and falling Log, use it to go to the lower level of the next plateau. Hit the exposed Switch Block and collect the Coins to the right and above, along with the 1-Up above. If you are the patient type, there's something else you can do here: before hitting the Switch Block, boot a Koopa Shell so that it bops between the Switch Block and the step to the right. Give it a little time, and the Shell will nail the big Boss Bass that comes up at you.

3/9: Eluding the Hanging Piranha Plant that comes charging from the first Pipe, watch out for the Bullet Bills and Bob-Ombs ahead. The fifth Block from the left of the overhead Ledge contains a power-up. The Ledge of ?'s ahead all have Coins. However, that's not what's important here: what matters are unlimited 1-Ups. Instead of killing the Koopa Paratroopa that comes at you at the very start of the level, grab its shell and, when you reach the second Cannon, throw the Shell down so it ricochets between it and the third Cannon—while you, looking to save your overalled self, hop onto the Ledge above the second Cannon . . . that is, the Ledge under the row of ?'s. The Shell will smack against Bullet Bills over and over, earning you points and then 1-Ups. You can also execute this maneuver by getting on top of the Pipe under the second Ledge of ?'s, allowing the Shell to rebound between the third Cannon and the Pipe. Don't go into the Pipe, but continue to the right. When you reach the

Ledge of Jump Blocks, use Blocks from its support
walls to kill Bob-Ombs, then get a power-up from
the leftmost Jump Block. Use a Bob-Omb to bash
through the next wall to the right, then jump up
against the leftmost breakable Block for a 1-Up.
Bust your way through the next set of Blocks to the
Pipe beyond. Descend, carrying a Koopa Shell or a
Block, if one's handy. You can use these against
your foes in the underwater realm. Otherwise, all
you need to know about the wet world is that if you
feel like taking a *loooong* swim, there's a Frog Suit
in the Pipe at the left end of this chamber. Incidentally, there's a way to turn Mario invisible in this
round—just for fun. (Certainly there's no strategic
value in having a Mario even you can't see!) Break
down the Block Wall just after the second Cannon,
then squat on the white Wall—the one before the
second Cannon—until you fall through. When you
touch down, hurry ahead to the Pipe: if it still looks
as though you're in the background as you descend,
you'll turn transparent. Like we said . . . it's wonderfully pointless!

World Three Ship: some new nemeses here are
Rocket Engines and reg'lar ol' Cannonballs. The
latter are actually quite useful, since you can jump
from one to the other as you travel. There are a lot
of Rocky Wrenches here, so you may be hitching a
ride on a lot of Cannonballs! When you face Wendy O.
Koopa, wait until she throws her first Candy Ring,
then jump on her head and hop to the right. When
she rises, slip underneath her to the left. Wait until
she throws the next Ring, and repeat. Do this one

more time, and she's headed for that great candy shop in the sky.

Giant Land

4/1: The giant world is fun. It's no more dangerous than previous worlds, and the oversized props are fun to look at, especially the big, lumbering Goombas. Getting under way: the first ? has a Coin, the second has a power-up. Destroy all the enemies in your way, then fly up to the top of the Pipe Waterfall. In the world above, enter the Pipe on the far left to access a super-secret bonus world where there are a pair of 1-Ups. Back on the ground, get a power-up from the next ? and a Coin from the Block beneath it. On the two-Block Ledge after the Clouds, hop right onto a Koopa and keep hitting successive Koopas without touching the Ledge. You'll earn 1-Ups as before.

4/2: The Pipes sink and rise in the water, but you've had experience with that and should get through with no sweat. When you come to the fifth Pipe—the one with the Blocks on it—use one to demolish the plant in the Pipe to your left, and throw another to the right to liberate the power-up from the ? Block. There's a Starman in the next ? (on the Ledge, just to the right of the exposed Switch Block). Make sure you activate the Switch Block, as collecting 22 Coins in this realm will enable you to get to the White House.

4/3: The Hammer Brothers will attack, one at a time, presenting little challenge: immediately after one jumps up and throws its Hammer, leap up and bash him. Enter the Pipe and you'll be in a world of darkness. It's an easy-to-clear place with Buzzies and their friends; nothing you can't handle. There are Coins in the first row of ?'s, and a power-up in the lone Block after the next Ledge. After you get this, start flying up to the right so you can reach the high Ledge which is covered with Coins. Dropping down the narrow chute on the right side, you'll land on a short slope. Kill the first Buzzy and kick it into the one on the right. Then get on top of the Ledge above and bop the Ledge over that one to release a 1-Up. Just be careful when you chase it to the right: Spiny is clinging to the ceiling up ahead, prepared to pounce. There's nothing to obtain beyond this point except Coins.

World Four Fortress: you'll be busy dodging everything from Hot Foot to Dry Bones, but there are three important things to remember. First, when you come to the Pipes, the third one from the left is the one you should enter to reach the underground chamber. Second, after entering that chamber, you'll find a power-up in the second ? from the right. Third, leave the chamber by uncovering the two Invisible Blocks in the vertical corridor at the end. Make sure, as you cause them to materialize, that you face Boo Diddly: that will tone down his aggressive tendencies.

4/4: Even if you don't have a Frog Suit, you can reap a good deal in this new water realm. As soon as you hit the churning waters, stand on the Ledge with the ?, get the power-up, and face left. Swim down slowly, making your way to the leftmost Pipe, and enter. It'll take some practice and skill to do this against the current, but it *can* be done. Inside, you'll find two rooms filled with Coins—well . . . they'll be filled with Coins after you trigger the Switch Blocks. When you emerge you'll be attacked by a Lakitu; the danger here is that the current might carry you right smack into a Spiny. There's nothing else to worry about in this realm.

4/5: Grabbing a Koopa, use it to smash the right side of the Pyramid; the ? has a power-up. After the Pipe, you'll face three Cannons in succession, each one higher than the one before it; as a result, Bullet Bills are plentiful. After the first Cannon, hit the middle ? of the Ledge above to get a power-up. The rest of the ?'s, and the ones in the next Ledge, are all Coins. You'll pass a Cloud with Coins over it, then a pair of Pipes and a clutch of Cannons; you're going to have to hop on top of a Bullet Bill in order to reach the lone Block overhead: bumping up against that Block will release a Vine, which will take you to a sky chamber. There, get the Tanooki Suit, activate the Switch Block, and collect the Coins that trail off into the skies. More Cannons and the Exit Pipe await on the ground.

4/6: Two important things in the first square of

Blocks overhead: a Starman and 1-Up. After you
get past the killer Plant in the first Pipe, you have
the option of entering the doorway beyond; do so,
and every foe in the giant world will become
normal-sized. The next ? has a power-up, and if you
opted to change everything to normal size, and you
fly into the sky here, you'll get Coins and a 1-Up
among the Clouds. On the ground there's a Starman in the second Block up of the Wall supporting
the Ledge; the Ledge itself will give you multiple
Coins. Jump up between the next two Pipes: there
are three Invisible Blocks here, all of them containing Coins. However, if you changed everything from
giant to small, one Block will give you a 1-Up. The
next door you encounter, like the first, will change
the size of everything in this realm.

World Four Fortress: this is the toughest and
most exciting fortress you've encountered thusfar!
The first chamber is similar to others in which
you've faced Dry Bones and had to cross Donut
Lifts. Get the power-up from the only ? here, and
don't stand on the Lifts too long: remember, they'll
fall if you do. Now, when you reach the bend in the
corridor—a reverse L—you'll find a Block. It's a
Switch Block: activate it, and a rectangle framed
by Coins will appear to the left. Step into the rectangle, press up on the controller, and you'll enter
an Invisible Doorway. Hop on the Arrow Lift and
head up—the Lifts move in whatever direction the
Arrow is pointing—but make sure you don't hit your
head on something while on this or *any* Lift. Do so,
and the Lift'll disappear. (*Why* is there a chance

that you'll bump your head? Because, fellow Mario-ites, you have to jump on some of the Lifts to get the Arrows to change direction.) This room is a vertical chamber, and you have to navigate your way through a maze of Pipes. Go up, right, switch Lifts and go up, hop to get the Lift to go left, go up, then get off the Lift and hop over the Pipe with the Piranha Plant to the downward-facing Pipe beyond. Enter, get the power-up from the ? above, go through the opening in the Pipes above, pass through the opening in the upper left, enter the break in the Ledge on the upper right, and exit via the Pipe. (If you're a little more adventurous, explore the Pipes here: never know when you might find secret rooms with Invisible Blocks, Coins, and 1-Ups!) Back in the main corridor, watch out for the Rotodisc as you advance, then brain Boom Boom three times as before.

World Four Ship: the last ship introduced the Bolt Lift, an optional, corkscrewing Elevator that will carry you safely through rough spots. It's here, too, and more useful than before; when you encounter it—over the Rocket Engines—jump on and keep hopping to move it ahead. To the right of the Bolt Lift is a ? with a power-up; another ?/power-up is located to the right of the Pipe at the end of the ship. Overall, this is actually a pretty simple level. All of the Cannons here are Rocket Engines, and as long as you proceed slowly, dashing ahead when each Rocket shuts down, you'll be okay. Watch out for the occasional Rocky Wrench. As for Iggy

Koopa—he's dogmeat if you hit him three times
outside of his Shell.

Sky Land

5/1: If you've gotten this far—more than halfway—
you don't need a blow-by-blow guide to the game.
Hereafter, we'll give you the high points. In this
realm, fly up and slightly to the right to enter the
Sky Pipe. Inside, there are two ways to go: squat
and leap and you'll enter a tight corridor that leads
to a Jump Block and the end of the realm. *Don't* go
that way. Take the lower route and you'll reach an
island where there are four 1-Ups. Don't forget to
fly skyward, activate the Switch Block, collect the
Coins, then bust your way out.

5/2: As you drop, use your tail—if you've got one,
obviously—to brake your descent. Hit the Jump
Blocks to get up to the Pipe—otherwise, you've got
a long and dangerous journey ahead of you, with
very few rewards. If you got up to the Pipe, enter
the next Pipe you encounter to access a room where
there are three 1-Ups.

5/3: This realm plays from right to left. Hiding just
beyond the second Pipe is a Goomba wearing the
poundiferous Kuribo's Shoe. Lure the Goomba back,
to the Ledge on the right, then jump up against the
Block on which it comes to rest. You'll get the Shoe,

and with it you can crush any foe. Even without it, there are no big surprises here.

World Five Fortress: break the first overhead Ledge and fly up. Head up and right to the Pipe. Enter, and follow the Arrow to fly up and uncover three Invisible Blocks containing 1-Ups. Thwomps and Rotodiscs are the foes here.

World Five Tower: more Thwomps and Rotos. When you reach the sky, the right block on each Tower is a Pile Driver Micro Goomba. After reentering the Tower and reemerging in the sky, get onto the Clouds under the four-Block Ledge. Hit the second Block from the left to activate a Vine, and climb to the next realm.

5/4: Fly up after the second Rotary Lift, so you can collect the Coins there. Don't get swallowed by the Waterfalls down below. Again, land on the fulcrum of each Rotary Lift for the most stable footing.

5/5: Kick away the Blocks on the second Pipe and enter for Coins and a Tanooki Suit. You'll be deposited near the end; there are power-ups in the top right Block of the overhead structure, and in the Block just beyond it, on the ground. If you didn't enter the Pipe, you can get the Coins below the Donut Lifts by standing on each Lift in turn, letting it drop, and collecting the Coin as it falls—making sure you jump off before it vanishes.

5/6: Jump onto Para-Beetles' backs to cross this realm. The only ? has a power-up.

5/7: Don't rush into this world: get a Starman on the Map. If you do so, you can obtain Starmen repeatedly to get you through the realm. You'll find them in the first, fourth, seventh, and eighth ?'s, the low Block on the other side of the next Wall, and the Block over the Pipe. If you enter the first Pipe, you'll find yourself in a world rich with goodies. Use a P-Wing to go to the top of the screen and hit the Switch Block; it's tough to do as plain old Raccoon Mario. Also, squat on the White Wall at the end until you drop through it. When you exit via the Pipe above, you'll have extended invincibility. Beware Micros on this level.

World Five Fortress: a Starman in the rightmost Block of the first Ledge of ?'s will help you. Raccoon Mario can fly through here, no trouble.

5/8: There's a power-up in the third ? from the left in the overhead Ledge. Get it: you'll need it to survive the Lakitu onslaught. The wisest tack here is to race—and we mean *race*—ahead rather than try to fight the rat: vantage points from which to jump down are much too few. You should take no more than 20 seconds to get through here. When you get to the Card section, wait: when Lakitu has tossed a quartet of Spinys, jump up and get the Card. You'll be rewarded with points *and* a 1-Up.

5/9: Fire Chomps chase you as you hop from vertically-moving Elevator to Elevator. If you're Raccoon Mario, fly above the Elevators, alighting only when necessary. This will give you the mobility you'll need to bop the Chomps.

World Five Ship: heavier artillery than usual here makes for a difficult passage. You'll certainly have to hop on Cannonballs and Bullet Bills to get through it. The boss here, Roy, doesn't jump in patterns like his fellow fiends, so you'll have to watch him. Keep your distance and leap only when he gives you an opening.

Ice Land

6/1: Ptooies make their debut here, but you can vault their Spiked Balls with ease. After the first Pipe, fly up to the doorway overhead. Enter, shimmy under the big Blocks, and hit the Switch Block. If you start this level with a Starman, you'll find another in the ? before the floating Coins.

6/2: The Clouds on this level shuttle back and forth like Elevators. Be careful not to get yourself trapped on the left side of a Ledge or Wall, especially when the screen begins moving upward, or you'll be scrolled off the screen.

World Six Fortress: stay on the Elevator here, or you'll never get across the Spikes. Watch out for the Rotodiscs during the vertical section of your Elevator trip. You can jump down this passage if you want, poising on the overhanging Wall and waiting until the Disc goes down. Enter the door at the end of the ride; reenter as often as you wish to reacquire the power-up in the ? Block.

6/3: You can run across gaps in the Columns by holding down the B button. On the L-shaped Ledge, hurl a Koopa at the floating Block ahead to activate a Vine. Climb and enter the Pipe.

6/4: The lone Block by the big Ice Wall has a 1-Up; hit the Block on the right so the Mushroom goes left, or you'll lose it. On the Elevator: as soon as it passes below the small Ice Wall, jump up to reveal an Invisible Jumping Block. Hop on for a trip to a Coin bank in the sky! Back on the ground, to the left of the icy runway is a Wall with a Switch Block. Activate it and run right—sliding *under* the Rotary Lift. Fly up to get to the 1-Up in the air.

6/5: Fly up after the ? to get to a Ledge with a 1-Up. Back on the ground, bust down all the Blocks on the straightaway *after* the slope, kill a Koopa, and fly up. At the right side of the Wall up above, toss the Shell against the Nipper Plants to destroy them. Enter the Pipe to leave. If you want a little more danger, don't fly up yet but continue right. The horizontal Pipe at the very end leads to a power-up room which you can exit and reenter as often as you wish.

6/6: Go down and get the Starman from the top Block on the rightmost of the two Walls. Beware the Cheep-Cheeps leaping from the Pools beyond.

In the water section, swim at once to the upper right for a 1-Up, then swim back down—this area is a dead end.

World Six Fortress: the Thwomps move from side to side here. They're easy to elude if you move cautiously. Boom Boom's pretty lethargic, making him easy to beat. The only ? here is a power-up.

6/7: The big challenge is negotiating all the Donut Lifts. Otherwise, there's not too much going on here. If you gather 78 Coins, the White Mushroom House will put in an appearance, so make that a goal. Only Fiery Mario can thaw the Coins at the end of the level.

6/8: Neat trick time: catch a Koopa right away, knock the Shell to the right, and run after it, pressing the B button. My, how the Nipper Plants will fall! When you come to the Ice Blocks later on, make sure you carry one to the Hill beyond to knock out more 'noying Nippers. Upon reaching the Switch Block, activate it, then use a P-Wing to fly up quickly and collect the 88 Coins in the sky. Incidentally, there's a totally useless trick you can do at the end of this level: there's a tunnel just before the Switch Block; enter with the P-Wing, and you can flutter underground to the left.

6/9: Go down the Pipe—there's nothing to the right worth getting. Swimming right, you can enter the first Pipe only if you're wearing a Frog Suit; inside are 35 Coins and a trio of 1-Ups. When you exit, swim up. Fly around the right side of the fat Wall above until you find a Switch Block. Activate it, and all the Munchers below will turn to Coins. Exit this realm via the last Pipe on the *top*.

6/10: After the second Pipe, cross the Ledge to the right and drop to the Blocks beyond it. Destroy Buster Beetle, then hit the Block on the right with an Ice Block and a Vine will sprout. Click on the Switch Block (far left) and the big batch of Blocks to the right will turn into a colossal collection of Coins. Fiery Mario can liberate tons of Coins back on the ground . . . but, more important, he can thaw the ice over a Pipe and get the Hammer Brothers Suit located inside. (This suit is not only useful in the fortress, but, if you squat while wearing it, the Piranha Plants can't harm you!)

World Six Fortress: either fly through this one in your Raccoon Suit or don the Hammer Suit so you can destroy Thwomps and Boo Diddlies. Speaking of Boo Diddly, if you face away from the creature it will attack . . . at which point you can spin suddenly and leap over it. When you cross the Conveyor Belt near Thwomp, unless you pelt the blockhead with Hammers, it'll be necessary to jump up and down—thus preventing yourself from moving ahead—until the big lunk moves. While you're doing this, be sure not to back into the Rotodisc! In the final room, pelt the Boo Diddlies with Hammers or simply evade them as the floor rises, bringing you to the door.

World Six Ship: take the high route so you can

collect the power-ups. You've been in spots like this before. As for Lemmy Koopa, get him between tosses of his Circus Balls.

Pipe Land

7/1: A big, busy vertical realm of Pipes is your introduction to this world, but apart from learning which one leads where, you won't have much trouble here. Get a power-up from the ? to the right of the Jump Block by killing a Koopa and tossing its Shell to the right of the ?. It'll ricochet back into the ?. Below the Pipe you're on there's an Invisible Block with a 1-Up, should you need it. Slightly above this section is a narrow Pipe, broken in the center. If you're Raccoon Mario, get rid of the Koopa—ditch it through the gap in the Pipes—go right, then run to the left, flying up to the Pipe below the Coin room. Enter to collect the riches.

7/2: Use a Frog Suit here. Descend via the second Pipe and swim left. Collect the Coins, then hit the Switch Block—don't do it the other way around! Swim hurriedly to the right to get the Coins before they revert to being Blocks. Exit via the last Pipe on the right, and jump up to uncover all the Jump Blocks. (Yes, we know you've covered your overhead exit. Never fear!) Go down the Pipe to the right, get the power-up on the left, go back up the Pipe, reenter the Pipe on the left, swim left, leave the water, and move overground, now, to the right.

Cross the bridge of Jump Blocks. (If it weren't here, you couldn't get over!) Enter the Pipe after the Jump Blocks, clear out the goodies down here, exit and leave the level using the fourth Block from the right at the end.

7/3: You can Starman your way through this level. Hit the first ? for a Starman, run using B button to the next Starman ? (leftmost of the four you'll encounter), rush ahead to the next identical setup for another Starman, and get the next one in the ? after the Pipe. There are two more Starmen in both Blocks on either side of the vertical Pipe. At the end of the level, use the B button to run right across the Pits ... including the humongous one at the end. Note: if you instinctively activate the Switch Block, you end your chances of getting all the Starmen. Also, if you hit a Starman Block when you're *not* invincible, all you'll get is Coins.

7/4: Before entering the Pipe to start, fly over the Wall for a pair of 1-Ups. Otherwise, this level is more of the familiar hijinks underwater. The one section that'll test your mettle is the Blooper field with Big Bertha roaming through it. You'll have to negotiate this dense region with quick, little movements.

7/5: When you go down the first Pipe after the Ledge, grab the Bob-Omb waiting down there and hurl it against the others coming from the right. That'll give you some breathing time. The interesting and challenging thing about this realm is the number of Invisible Blocks you encounter. Jump up in virtually any gap and you'll find one; it's fun but, obviously, you don't want to box yourself into an area. Before you bop, make sure there's a back door! At the end of the level, you have to uncover all of the Invisible Blocks to build a bridge by the L-shaped Ledge. Otherwise, you can only get out if you're Raccoon Mario.

Piranha Garden: Piranha Plants infest this level. There are two sections. In the first, cross the Pipes by taking small hops from Pipe to Pipe, moving to each new one as the Plant there is going down. (Some players prefer big, fat B button leaps . . . but those are a little reckless compared to little steps which allow you to plan each one.) In either case, a misstep and Mario is Plant food! In the next section of Pipes 'n' Piranha Plants, the first Jump Block contains a Starman. When you reach the three Pipes at the end, take the one in the middle to get out.

World Seven Fortress: first, go up on the silvery-blue Ledge, go right, and uncover the Switch Block. That'll turn every Block in this library of Blocks into a Coin. When you're done, take the door on the Ledge, go right and down the Pipe, claim the Tanooki Suit, and enter the horizontal Pipe at the end. Collect the bonuses in this room. Exit using the door at the bottom left, and reenter as often as you wish to replenish your power-ups. When you're through, leave via this bottom left door and head left. Go past the door and fly up. Enter the Pipe in the ceiling to battle the Boomster.

7/6: This one's fun . . . but frustrating when you're first getting to know the ropes. First, it's full of those multidirectional Lifts identical to those in the World Four Fortress—the ones you jump on to change direction. Only not all of them change when you leap. A few key strategies: the second Lift you'll use passes some Spike-covered Ledges. To get by the two Ledges, switch sides on the Lift as it passes the Ledge. You can—and should!—pass through the first vertical Pipe you encounter flush against the right wall. When you ride your Lift past the Piranha Plants in the Pipes on top, simply shift to the opposite side of the Lift to escape the carnivores' teeth.

7/7: If you're not Raccoon Mario, you can get across the sea of Munchers here by using Starmen. There are four ? Blocks, each with a Starman: liberate the pointy helpers as you pass the Block and run after the Starman . . . but *don't* catch it until your present dose of invincibility is about to wear out. Otherwise, you won't have enough Starman power to get you all the way to the end.

7/8: Fireballs are *really* useful against the Piranha Plants here. If you don't have it, watch your step. There's a Starman in the leftmost ? atop the gray Wall—after the second downward-facing Pipe. Jump up along the right side of the third downward-facing

Pipe—the one over the white Wall—to reveal an Invisible Jump Block. Get on it to vault to a celestial bank! Shortly beyond that Block, you'll find three pipes together: a tall one to the right of a pair of squat ones. When the Ptooie retreats, go down the leftmost Pipe to get a Hammer Brothers Suit.

7/9: This one's a maze, and the clock's your real enemy here. Here's the route: go up at the Jump Blocks, up/left through the gap, up/right through the next gap, then left through two Walls and up the gap to the left of the second Wall. Rush along the top, cross the two Ledges, stay on the top until you reach the Jump Blocks, then drop to the left of them, go through the Wall, go up/left through the gap, through the next Wall to the left, down, right, down, right—under the Ledge of ?'s—up/right through the gap, go through two Walls to the right, go up the Ledges, right across the Pipe, through the Wall, down and left through the Wall, down through the gap, right through the Wall, up/right through the gap, then right and down. Enter the Pipe to leave. Stop and hit ?'s *only* if there's time.

World Seven Fortress: this is a museum of menace, with all the worst foes. If you have a Raccoon or Hammer Brothers Suit—wear it. There's a Starman in the first Block—after the third Pipe. Enter the last Pipe on the right—beneath the overhang—to meet the boss.

World Seven Ship: to go from platform to platform here, use Raccoon Mario *or* press the B button when you jump. Otherwise, the only way to cross the ship is by using the troublesome Bolt Lifts.

Dark Land

Tanks: you must battle increasingly larger Tanks in this level. One key to surviving is to leap off each successive Tank when the tip of the barrel of the next Tank appears on the right. The second-to-last Tank has two Cannons for a double attack; get on top of the upper barrel as quickly as possible.

Battleships: there's a 1-Up to be had on the right side of the first Mast. Don't jump up to get it, though, until the Cannon behind has fired! The important, secret strategy to master here is learning how to swim beneath the Battleships. It's difficult, but it can be done.

Hand Attack: as you cross the Bridges here, giant hands will shoot up to grab you. They're not *too* tough to avoid. If you let them grab you, you'll be taken to secret worlds; not bad if you're a skilled player and can fight your way out. The rewards are worthwhile.

Airships: if you're not Raccoon Mario, have Hammers or fireballs to take out the Rocky Wrenches. It's best to position yourself on the Rocket Engine when jumping to the next Airship.

8/1: Fly up; the Switch Block will fill the air below with Coins. The fifth (super-tall) Pipe contains three 1-Ups.

8/2: Enter the quicksand, enter one of the Pipes, and you'll pop up right near the end of the level.

World Eight Fortress: this is a realm of secret doors which will really power you up! When you reach the Blocks forming a big H, activate the Switch Block on top. Enter the door below it, and you'll access a secret room and a 1-Up. After you're attacked by a trio of Thwomps, go up the Staircase and continue right. After the second window, you'll find a Switch Block; hit it, head left, go in the door, go down and left and into another door. The leftmost of the three Blocks contains a 1-Up. On the bottom level of the Fortress, the door below the Thwomp allows for repeated entry and, thus, multiple power-ups. Toward the end of the lower level, climb the Staircase and continue ahead to two Blocks underfoot. The right Block contains a Switch Block. Hit it for access to the power-up on the upper floor.

Super Tank: in general, stay roughly one-quarter screen length from the right, so you can deal *immediately* with what's ahead. Rocky Wrench traffic is heavy here, so be ready to make quick, short moves back or ahead to dodge the homicidal handymen.

Koopa Castle: beware the Statues here—they fire lasers. As you make your way through the maze of the Castle, always take the high path when you have a choice. When you reach Bowser, the tack to take is simple: let him kill himself! Stand on the third Block in from the left, let him jump at you, and scurry to the same position on the right. His leap will dig a pit. He'll jump after you at your new position, digging a new pit; when he leaps, you simply run into the first pit he dug. He'll jump after you; get up and out of the way *fast*, and he'll land in the pit, digging it deeper. Repeat this process over and over until he digs his way through the six layers of Blocks to the bottom of the screen . . . and death.

DR. MARIO

Objective:

Dr. Mario—helpful as ever—is busy flinging Vitamins into a Medicine Bottle. Your task is to eliminate Viruses in the Bottle by placing those Vitamins on or beside them. Your goal is to stack three Vitamin-segments on or directly below the Viruses which are the *same color* as the germ—or lay them beside the Virus, forming a row of four like-colored segments. If you interrupt the stack or row with another color, you'll have to stack three matching colors on or beside the *new* Vitamin section in order to eliminate it and regain access to your original stack or row. The stage ends when all the Viruses have been eliminated *or* if there's a Vitamin bottleneck in the Bottleneck and Dr. Mario can't throw any more in! Each stage has more Viruses than the one before it; there are twenty stages of difficulty; in the NES version, when you complete the twentieth level, a Bottle with the same

number of Viruses (in a different pattern, of course)
appears as the twenty-first and then upwards. (Unfortunately, if you lose on twenty-one, you get
booted back to twenty. There's no way to hang on
to any subsequent level.) When you beat level
twenty in the Game Boy version, you see the viruses floating in what looks like water with some
kind of kelp growing next to them. We can tell you
how to win, but we have *no* idea what the defeated
germs are doing taking a bath at the bottom of the
sea. (Or is that supposed to be a bloodstream? With
plants?) Perhaps they're waiting to make a come-
back in *Super Mario Bros. 4*?

Gameplay:

In the NES version, the Vitamins are either solid
blue, red, or yellow, or various two-tone combinations thereof. In the Game Boy edition, they're solid
black, white, and gray, or combinations of those.
Once the Vitamin is thrown, you must decide
whether to let it fall the way it was tossed (that is,
lengthwise) or whether you want it to drop so that
it's standing on-end. You can rotate the Vitamin,
speed up its descent, and/or shift it from side to side
as it drops. Once the Vitamin touches down, you
have exactly *one second* to shift it left or right as
far as you want, stand it upright, flip it over entirely—or any mixture of those moves! When you
stack or line up a Virus and three matching colors,
or four matching Vitamin segments, all will vanish. If a solid-colored Vitamin is placed on three

other segments—thus completing the row or stack with five segments in all—all five will disappear. In the very neck of the bottle, even if that topmost (fifth) segment of the stack is a different color than the other four, it, too, will disappear. A Vitamin can be left hanging: if you put one side lengthwise on a vertical stack, only that end needs to be supported. The other section can hang over empty space, and other Vitamins can be piled on *it.* These hanging segments and anything you've placed on them will drop if the supporting stack is eliminated; if, in falling, that section (or sections) completes a stack or row below, it too will vanish. Fortunately, while all of this is going on, the Viruses do nothing but sit still and glow ominously. *Note:* in the following discussion, "stack" means a vertical collection of segments, while "row" refers to a horizontal collection. *Another*—albeit less important—*note*: in the NES game, try not to be distracted by the sound the Vitamin segments make when a row or stack is completed and other sections drop. (The falling Vitamin(s) sounds just like the "nyuk, nyuk, nyuk" made by Curly Howard of the Three Stooges!)

Points:

You earn points for making Viruses disappear, not for placing Vitamins on the screen or getting rid of rows or stacks which consist solely of Vitamin segments.

Strategies:

There are no specific strategies to apply on a screen-by-screen basis, since every screen is different and the sequence of the Vitamins you're offered changes from game to game. Here, then, are general tactics:

*The Vitamins always enter the Bottle facing the same way Dr. Mario is holding them. This is useful to know, just in case you have to slide one somewhere or flip one on-end in a hurry.

*Because Vitamins can be shifted even after they've touched down, don't jump the gun on the Vitamin waiting in the "batter's box." By trying to move that one the instant it enters the Bottle, you may accidentally shift the previous Vitamin which hasn't quite settled in yet.

*Likewise, don't "overflip" a Vitamin. Many players tend to hold their finger on the button, lifting it when the Vitamin's been turned the way they want it. *Don't*. If you hold it one moment longer than necessary, the Vitamin will turn again . . . and not in any way that'll help you. This is especially deadly when, in early stages of later rounds, you're sliding Vitamins into the corner. If you meant to place a Vitamin down flat, and it winds up on-end, it may reach the top and block your access to the side of the screen.

*Always look at what's coming next: it'll influence what you do *now*. For example, if you see that your present piece will clear a row or stack and allow you to reach a Virus that the next Vitamin will remove (or bring closer to removal), take advantage of that.

*At the beginning in the higher levels, when you get solid-toned Vitamins, try to place them upright on the Viruses closest to the Bottleneck first, especially if there are two already in a stack or row. You'll want to get those out of the way to give yourself some elbow room.

*If you only need *one* more section to fill up a row of four, think about whether it's better to place the Vitamin on its side or on-end: you might be able to start a new row or stack with the other section of the Vitamin. (Remember: when a stack vanishes, there are often Viruses underneath waiting to be built-upon. Many players tend to overlook those, completing stacks by laying Viruses lengthwise.)

*Before adding a solid-tone Vitamin on three pre-existing row or stack segments—as mentioned earlier, causing all *five* portions to disappear—see if you can use that fifth piece on the side to start a new row or stack. There's no reason to waste a segment just because it's easier to get rid of the whole Vitamin! By the same token, eliminate that extra piece if, in falling, it'll block access to a pair or threesome of segments.

*If you have a choice of two or more rows or stacks in the Bottle which can be eliminated with a particular Vitamin, go for them in this order: highest with a Virus; highest without a Virus; lowest with a Virus. As mentioned above, it's important to keep the top of the Bottle clear so you can maneuver.

*If you have a Vitamin and no exposed matching tone on which to drop it, place it in a row without a Virus. Otherwise, you'll simply add to the length of time you need to get to the Virus (unless two solid Vitamins are coming in a row, in which case you can simply use the second to eliminate the first.)

*Pursuant to the above, in the later stages it's imperative to create safe "corridors" in which you can deposit unwanted Vitamins. The last thing you want is to bury Viruses *deeper* as the Vitamins speed up. Having a corridor like that serves another purpose as well: you can use two-tone Vitamins more efficiently. Assume that the last corridor on the right is safe, and the next stack to the left has a blue (or gray) Virus on top. You can place a blue and red and then a blue and yellow Vitamin on the blue Virus (or gray and white and then gray and black on the gray Virus) without worrying how the different, unused Vitamin halves are stacking up in that far right corridor. Needless to say, it's even better to have safe corridors on either side of a Virus: that way, you can drop the unused half of two-tone Vitamins on matching segments, eliminating them rather than piling them up in a multi-toned heap on one side.

If you don't have a safe corridor or two in later stages, *never* stack two-tone Vitamins together if they have only one color in common. In other words, if you have a red and yellow Vitamin (or gray and black), followed by a red and blue (or gray and white) Vitamin, don't match the reds (or grays) up, leaving the other segments hanging off the sides. When you finally eliminate the red or gray, you'll have all those other segments to deal with—not an appealing prospect when Vitamins are raining like confetti! You can, however, stagger Vitamins this way in early stages: when the center stack vanishes, it'll dump both sides, enabling you to finish them off. For instance, if you have four yellows (or grays) in the center, you'll have, at worst, two blues (or blacks) and two reds (or whites) on the sides . . . not a daunting prospect, especially if, in falling, they land on matching Vitamin segments of Viruses.

*Don't forget that you can attack a Virus from underneath. If there's an open passage to the bottom, you can slide a Vitamin *under* a previously placed Vitamin which may be blocking off a Virus. When doing this, you should watch for open sections where you can place a solid-colored Vitamin upright to finish a stack.

*In the later rounds, where Vitamins come faster and the Viruses are more plentiful, try to build rows rather than stacks. If you have no immediate need for a tone, put it *beside* one just like it—flat if it's a solid Vitamin (and if there's room), on-end if it's two-tone. Spaces may open up on either side, suddenly making it possible for you to build a horizontal row of four or more.

*If there are isolated Viruses high on the screen, and you can't pile Vitamins on top, don't leave the Virus there! More games are lost because of these hermit Viruses. Stack Vitamins one atop another to build up to them and eliminate them. This is easier to do when the Vitamins are coming at you slowly, in the early going. Obviously, when build-ing up like this, make sure you stack *different* toned Vitamins on top of each other; if you stack the same tones on each other, they'll just keep vanishing when you've got four of them!

*One way of reaching those isolated Viruses is to build bridges (more accurately, staircases) across large gaps. Lay a Vitamin down flat, place another one flat on top of it, so that half of it is hanging over empty space; drop the next one on top of that Vitamin—also flat so that half of *it* is hanging over—and so on. The whole shebang will resemble a staircase and will enable you, for example, to drop a solid-colored Vitamin horizontally beside two oth-ers in an upper corner or cut a section from the middle of a tall multi-colored stack. When it comes time to eliminate the staircase, you can use each successively lower "step" to create rows with the Vitamin above it.

*In levels nineteen and twenty, if you can't open the stage by creating a stack or row of three or four, shove the Vitamin off to the side (obviously, on a matching tone) rather than dropping it in the cen-ter. You can always get rid of "side clutter" later by creating rows or building up to the higher seg-ments, as described above. But if you let isolated stacks of two (a Virus and one matching Vitamin part) collect in the middle, they'll pile up fast, and the round will end before you know it!

*If you can slide a Vitamin into a stack vertically (that is, the Vitamin lying on its side), it's possible to take out up to eight segments of Vitamin and

Virus at once by completing two pre-existing sets of three. Unfortunately, the game won't let you take out more than that (meaning you can't use one piece to finish a stack above and below *and* a row to the side.)

*Whenever possible, create several stacks, one for each of the identical two-tone Vitamins. It's easier to handle them when you know ahead of time where they're going—and, after you have just four of them, they'll disappear!

*Want to set up a row, but you don't have the support underneath? Consider the following. You may not be able to place a solid-tone Vitamin right next to the Virus or segment you want to take out. However, you might be able to put it horizontally on a support-segment *two* places over. What you'll have, then, is the Virus, a gap, and the solid-tone Vitamin. All you need to do to create a row, then, is to drop enough Vitamins into the gap to fill it, enabling you to reach the level of the three in the row you're building. When the right colored segment comes along, slip it into the gap on-end.

*It isn't as important in the early stages, but it's vital in the later stages: Vitamins which stand on-end so that one segment is *completely* out the top of the bottle only count as *one* segment. So don't plan on making that row of two disappear with a one-tone Vitamin: the game will read it as three segments, not four.

*In later stages, if you end up with a stack of three Vitamin segments and/or Viruses piled on the far left or right, with just one space between them and the top of the Bottle, it's often very difficult to slide a Vitamin on top of them. What to do? Using the same tones, build a stack of three right beside it. When a solid-tone Vitamin comes along, slide it over and eliminate both stacks. The addition of the extra stack gives you a place to "land" the solid-tone Vitamin before it falls, after which you can slide it into place.

*Suppose you have a stack of two matching segments being held up by a stack where there are three matching segments. For example, three blues (or grays) in the center and two reds (or whites) to the left. Suppose, further, that there's a gap beneath the reds (or whites), below which there's another red (or white). A solid red (or white) Vitamin comes down. *Don't* put it on the two reds (or whites). That will eliminate them needlessly. Use the solid red (or white) Vitamin somewhere else, wait until you can get rid of the stack of blue (or gray), and let the reds (or whites) to its left *drop* on the red (or white) segment or Virus below. All you need is one more red (or white) to get rid of the stack. Had you eliminated the two reds (or whites) with the solid Vitamin, you'd have been left with the one red (or white) exposed after eliminating the blue (or gray) stack . . . and nothing useful on top of it.

*Don't get smug when you've got the Viruses way down on level twenty. You'll be surprised how fast the unused Vitamins pile up! Players (this one included) have lost with just *one* Vitamin left on the screen 'cause it got buried!

*Eventually, players who make it to the end of

the later rounds will be faced with the following dilemma: there's a Vitamin on its way down which can be used to eliminate a row or stack containing a Virus, *or* can knock out a row or stack comprised solely of Vitamin parts—but which, when eliminated, will expose a Virus which is the only one of its color left on the screen. In this case, go for the latter: exposing a new Virus will give you one more useful place to put falling Vitamins.

*When trying to build rows, notice that you can drop a stack in order to shift a high segment in that stack to a point where it will add to or complete your row.

AFTERWORD

Hope you enjoyed this trip through all five Mario-lands.

Many of you have written asking about a tip we gave in *How to Win at Nintendo Games* #1, about the mysterious "water world" at the end of 1–2 in *Super Mario Bros.*

Most of you say it doesn't work for you.

Well . . . it doesn't always work for us either! We don't know why, but that's one of the mysteries of Mario, we guess.

While we're on the subject, here's another tip that has worked at the same spot—though, again, not every time: if you face the left side of the screen, jump up and break all of the Blocks on top *except* the one next to the Pipe, you can also reach the wet world by walking through the wall.

Give it a try. Then write, in care of the publisher, to let us know how you make out!

In fact, many readers have written with comments about our previous Nintendo Games books. Though there isn't space to acknowledge all of the correspondents, a few whose letters were particularly interesting are: Eric Acosta, Tony Basso, Ken Bowen, Jason Bustard, Charlie Davis, John Detroy, John Doty, Darren Ebert, Sean Fain, Chris Federowicz, Bree Frick, Bo Hakala, Scott Hanlin, Daniel Healy, Fayaz Jamal, Chris Katides, Michael S. Kugelman, Joey Lee, Keith Lock, Jeffrey Lubick, James McIntire, Chris Mapes, Eric Medley, Joy Moorman, Kyle Orwig, Jon Peaslee, Bo Pedersen, James Picou, Kevin Preusse, Brian Richards, Donna Roberts, Jesse Rowlett, Jason Schneider, David Schoenberger, Tom Schrantz, Jack Small, Gregory Alan Smith, Mary K. Spencer, Jim Thompson, and Sarah Whitlock.

Deepest thanks of all to some highly-treasured readers: Jeremy Cate, Alan Fuller, Tony Rizzo, Jan Walpole, and Laura Wood.

See you all in the next book. Until then, happy videogaming!

Sports Immortals

FROM ST. MARTIN'S PAPERBACKS

MAGIC AND THE BIRD
Magic Johnson and Larry Bird
by Mitchell Krugel
_____ 91725-2 $3.95 U.S.   _____ 91726-0 $4.95 Can.

THE WIT AND WISDOM OF YOGI BERRA
by Phil Pepe
_____ 91760-0 $3.95 U.S.   _____ 91761-9 $4.95 Can.

WAYNE GRETZKY
by Stephen Hanks
_____ 91779-1 $3.95 U.S.   _____ 91780-5 $4.95 Can.

MICHAEL JORDAN
by Mitchell Krugel
_____ 91697-3 $3.95 U.S.   _____ 91698-1 $4.95 Can.

DON BAYLOR
by Don Baylor with Claire Smith
_____ 92106-3 $4.95 U.S.   _____ 92107-1 $5.95 Can.

HOW TO
WIN
AT
NINTENDO
GAMES

Jeff Rovin

The Nintendo videogame system is the ultimate in home entertainment—an unrivaled source of excitement and challenge. And *How to Win at Nintendo Games* can help you get to the top of your form! Now packed with more vital information than ever, the new updated and expanded edition of *How to Win at Nintendo Games* covers all of your favorite games!

How to Win at Nintendo Games is an unofficial guide—not endorsed by Nintendo®. Nintendo is a registered trademark of Nintendo of America Inc.